ON THE LONG MARCH
WITH CHAIRMAN MAO

On the Long March
with
Chairman Mao

Chen Chang-feng

University Press of the Pacific
Honolulu, Hawaii

On the Long March with Chairman Mao

by
Chen Chang-Feng

ISBN:0-89875-405-4

University Press of the Pacific
Honolulu, Hawaii
http://www.universitypressofthepacific.com

Contents

Early Days

I was born in the village of Lingnao, in Ningtu County, Kiangsi Province in the autumn of 1915. Ours was a very poor family. When I was eleven, mother died. My father supported the family by working for the landlords. Because of our poverty and the oppression we suffered at the hands of the landlords and local despots, I have hated this rapacious class of exploiters from the bottom of my heart ever since I was a child.

In 1928 our village suddenly buzzed with talk about a "Red Army" that had appeared in the nearby village of Wangfang as if from nowhere. It was passing Ningtu, heading for Juichin and Tapoti. This news stirred the whole village, and as it spread around, it took on the proportions of a legend. The poor were glad. They said these troops helped the poor. They were called the Communist Party or the Red Army, they would square accounts with the rich and throw the gold and silver of the landlords and despots on the streets so that

1

the poor could pick it up for themselves. The rich were scared. They called these men cut-throats and bandits. I was only thirteen at the time. I knew nothing of politics, but I agreed immediately with what the poor people said. Those few words: "Down with the rich! Up with the poor!" burned themselves into my memory.

Several days passed. Some of the village pedlars who had been to Changting in Fukien Province gleefully recounted what they had seen. The Red Army had captured Changting, fought the local despots and overthrown the landlords. The poor were given land; now they were standing on their feet for the first time.

This news made me happy and I waited impatiently for the day when these soldiers of the poor would come to our village.

That New Year's Eve our house was searched and ransacked. We owed the local despot some money, and everything we owned — from the tiny plot of land on the wild heath to the tattered quilt in my room — was taken away. It was only thanks to the neighbours who begged pity for us that we were left a single broken saucepan for cooking rice in. Our life became harder than ever. Luckily I got jobs herding cattle for other people. But I lived worse than the animals. When an ox or a horse finishes its work, it gets its fodder, but sometimes our whole family starved with not even a drop of gruel between us.

What should I do? Join the Red Army! The idea suddenly came into my mind, and the more I thought about it, the more determined I was to do it. Just after the New Year the night of the second day of the First Moon was pitch-black. I and a neighbour, a youngster named Wen, slipped out of the village secretly without even telling our families and headed for Changting. We were determined to find and join the Red Army.

We travelled on for I don't know how many days or how far without meeting a single Red Army soldier. We were famished but never thought of turning back. On a hill about fifteen *li*[1] from Changting we came upon two soldier sentries with red stars on their caps. The Red Army at last! We immediately went up to them and declared that we had come to join the Red Army. After questioning us in detail, they pointed to Changting and told us that if we wanted to enlist, we should go there to the Red Recruiting Corps.

At Changting we found the Red Recruiting Corps stationed by a stone bridge. We were so happy that we wanted to join right away, without even listening to their explanations. We never expected that after going into our cases they would shake their heads and say "No". I was too young and could hardly shoulder a rifle, they said. Tears came to my eyes. But I wouldn't give up. "I must join the Red Army!" I cried out. "If you don't let me join, I'll stay right here where I am!" At last, seeing that I was so set, they relented, and ever since that day I have been a member of our glorious people's army.

I was posted as a bugler with the headquarters of the Fourth Army of the Chinese Workers' and Peasants' Red

---

[1] A *li* is approximately one-third of a mile

Army, under the command of Comrade Chu Teh. Later I became an orderly. One afternoon at the end of March 1930, when the headquarters was in Paisha Village, Yung-feng County, Kiangsi, Adjutant Officer Liu told me that I would be transferred. At that time I did not fully understand the meaning of the word "transferred". So I asked him what it meant.

"Transferred means that you'll change your place of work," said Liu, looking at me intently as if there were something important which he could not tell me at once.

"Where'll I be transferred to?" I asked Liu again. I wasn't too pleased because I was well satisfied where I was.

"You'll go to the Front Committee as orderly for Commissar Mao," he said with a smile.

I knew the Front Committee of the Chinese Communist Party, but who Commissar Mao was, I wasn't quite clear. He must be a leading officer, I reckoned, otherwise he couldn't have an orderly. But what sort of man was he? Was he good tempered?

Adjutant Liu, seeing my hesitation, patted me on the shoulder and said encouragingly: "You're a lucky little devil. Commissar Mao is a wonderful man. You'll certainly have a wonderful future if you work with him!" Then he handed me a letter of introduction, told me to pack up my things and be off. I had little to carry. All I had weighed just about three catties[1] all told.

The Front Committee was in the same village, so I was soon there. I was a bit nervous. A comrade named Wu

---

[1] A catty is equal to about 1 1 lb

took me to the Commissar. He lived in a typical Kiangsi wooden house with two rooms, one a bedroom and the other an office. We entered through the bedroom. In it was an ordinary wooden bed covered with a cotton sheet. It didn't even have a pillow. I grew less nervous. Judging from the room, the Commissar must be living as simply as all of us, I thought. Two men were talking together in the office. Comrade Wu indicated the man in the chair and whispered: "That's Commissar Mao." I looked at him curiously. His grey uniform was the same as ours. The only difference was that the pockets on his coat seemed to be especially large. His black hair contrasted sharply with his fair complexion. Maybe he was a bit too thin. His eyes seemed to be very big and keen. He seemed to be about forty at most. Talking to a man opposite him, he gesticulated with his hands; his voice was gentle. Although I didn't understand what he was talking about, I felt he was very sincere. A little time later, his visitor stood up to go. He too stood up. It was only then that I saw he was quite tall. As soon as the visitor went out, Comrade Wu said to Commissar Mao, pointing at me, "I have found an orderly for you."

Although I felt a bit shy, I didn't forget the manners which I had learned at army headquarters. I advanced a step, saluted and said "Report!" in a loud voice. Commissar Mao looked at me and smiled kindly. That smile swept away all my reservations.

"What's your surname?" he asked.

"Chen," I replied loudly, like a real soldier.

"What are you called?"

"Chang-feng."

"How old are you?"

"Sixteen." By this time my voice sounded a bit more natural.

"Why did you join the Red Army?" Commissar Mao asked me like a school teacher questioning a pupil.

"The Red Army is good. It fights the local despots!" I was still standing straight at attention. Commissar Mao made me sit down and asked with interest, "Are there local despots in your home village?"

"Yes," I said, "I was driven away by them myself."

And I told him in detail how I had lived with my family and how I had run away and joined the Red Army. He listened to me attentively, sometimes nodding and smiling slightly. This put me at ease, and I felt I could get along with this man very well; so I talked on at great length. It was only when Comrade Wu nudged me that I realized I had talked too long. I felt a bit embarrassed and stopped.

"Well," said Commissar Mao. "Now you'll have to work and study hard." After a pause, he asked, "Can you write your name?"

I stood up and twisted the edge of my jacket in embarrassment. "I've never been to school. I don't know how to write," I replied.

Commissar Mao smiled and stood up.

"Then you'll have to learn to write — your own name and the names of other people. You'll like that, won't you?"

"Yes, I will," I replied in a low voice.

He turned and addressed Comrade Wu.

"This is a new comrade, you must do your best to help him." Then he turned back to me, "If there is anything you're not clear about, just ask them."

As I went down the stairs with Comrade Wu, he said to me:

"Why did you gabble on so? Don't you know how busy he is?"

I shook my head.

"He's a busy man," Wu continued. "Remember not to make a noise when he's reading. Besides he always works late into the night. You must get him his breakfast, but not too early, mind!"

"Yes," I replied.

I was very happy and so excited that I didn't sleep a wink the whole night.

The next morning I took a wooden bucket to fetch water which I took to be my daily routine. I was stopped by Comrade Wu.

"What are you doing?"

"Fetching water for Commissar Mao," I said confidently.

"Didn't I tell you Commissar Mao slept late?" Wu was impatient. "You're not to wake him up!"

I nodded and put down the bucket.

For some days after that I would set Commissar Mao's washing water for him by his door early in the morning without making a sound and then sit in a small hammock near the landing waiting there for his orders. But Commissar Mao rarely called me and I sat in this way for several days.

One day after washing, however, he asked me:

"Chen Chang-feng, why do you always sit there without stirring?"

I held the hammock still and answered, "I am afraid if I go away you'll not find me if you want me."

He smiled as if talking to a child. "From now on you must not just sit there doing nothing. When there is nothing for you to do here, you go and study with the others. There isn't much for you to do here."

At that time battles were being fought every day. We were constantly on the move. We'd seldom stay at a place for more than a month.

Commissar Mao's life was very simple and I soon got to know his habits. His personal possessions included only two blankets, one cotton sheet, two grey uniforms, just as we privates wore, a worn overcoat, and one grey woollen sweater. Then he had a broken umbrella, a bowl for eating and a knapsack with nine compartments for his maps, documents and books. When we were campaigning or on the march, he carried the knapsack and umbrella himself. I would carry the rest. When we came to our camp site, I would find two wooden boards, put them together and spread the blankets and sheet on them, folding up his uniforms to make a pillow. This was his bed.

He slept very little. We had a small lamp; during the march this was used as a torch to light the way, but when in camp it was set on a brick or stone for use in his office.

After supper he would light this lamp, open up his knapsack and take out his maps, documents and books, papers, and writing brush and sometimes work till dawn.

At that time I was a youngster and couldn't sit up all night without sleep. When Commissar Mao was reading or writing, I would sit beside him, but very soon I'd doze off snoring away with my head on his desk. We would both smile whenever he woke me up and told me to go to bed.

On summer nights he would ask me to fetch some water.

Then I'd take the little wooden dipper and bring some cold water. Because we didn't have a basin, he would soak the towel in the dipper and rub his face and sometimes his body to freshen himself up. Then he'd feel hungry, and I'd warm up the "rice sandwich" (two layers of rice with cooked vegetables in between) left in the bowl since the afternoon for him to eat.

Sometimes he couldn't finish his bowl of rice so I would cover it up with a piece of paper for him to eat at the next meal. Once I threw away the rice he had left and the next day he asked:

"Chen Chang-feng, where is the rice I left yesterday?"

I told him what I had done and he criticized me.

"There is a struggle for every grain of rice that the people grow. In future you mustn't throw away what I leave. Keep it for the next meal."

At one time we were marching and fighting every day. Commissar Mao did not even have time to get a sip of hot water. I grew worried. So I was always trying to get a thermos bottle for him. Often we captured a place and war booty came to us, but Commissar Mao never kept anything. He would always send what he got to his subordinates or the hospital. In the winter of 1931, when we captured Chian in Kiangsi, I found a thermos bottle there in the house of a local despot who had run away. I was overjoyed at this stroke of luck but I was afraid the Commissar would find out about it. On the march I used to get someone else to carry it for me so that he would not know about it. With that bottle I was always able to keep some hot water ready for him, but it was still difficult to prepare him a quick meal. His small bowl could not hold very much rice. It was enough for a supper, but on the march it was not of much use. Often we would be on the march again immediately after a battle. Then when we took a rest and ate our meal, Commissar Mao would still have to eat his cold "sandwich".

In November 1931, the Central Workers' and Peasants' Democratic Government was founded in Juichin and he was elected Chairman of the Republic. That's when we began to call him Chairman instead of Commissar Mao. But he still used his little bowl at meals. It was only in February 1934, when we captured Changchow, Fukien, that I managed to find a real three-decker enamel container for his food.

A Visit Home

WHENEVER we captured a county seat or town, Chairman Mao would send people or go himself to the local government office to get enemy documents and archives, and then to the local post-office to buy newspapers and magazines. Often we'd go with empty hands and come back loaded with packages of books and magazines. In the evening, Chairman Mao would mark them with red pencil so that we could clip and keep what was needed.

One day we came to Hsinfeng County, Kiangsi. We had been there several times before, so the local people knew the Red Army. All the shops were open and many people came out to welcome us. As soon as we settled down in our billet, Chairman Mao called me: "Come, Chen Chang-feng! To the post-office!"

To my mind at that time a post-office was just a shop for buying and selling books.

11

When we got there Chairman Mao began to browse through the piles of books and papers. Sometimes he would pick one up and hand it to me. We had paid for what we wanted and when I was packaging up our purchases I asked him: "Chairman Mao, what does a post-office do?"

"Oh, they do a lot of things," he answered. "They deliver letters and newspapers; handle telegrams and telephone calls. If you want to send a letter home, they'll send it for you."

If I write a letter, could they really take it all the way home for me? I wondered.

As we left the post-office, the thought of this preoccupied my mind. I thought it was a wonderful thing. I hadn't been home for two or three years now; I didn't know how my father was or even if he were still alive. . . . Many questions flashed through my mind. It would be fine if I could send a letter home!

When we came back to our billet it was already dusk. I put down the books and papers and lit the lamp for Chairman Mao, who immediately began to read. It was time for me to get the supper but I couldn't get the post-office out of my head. I stood there day-dreaming.

"What's wrong?" Chairman Mao asked me, noticing my worried look.

"Chairman Mao," I said, "can they really send a letter home?"

"Whom do you mean?" he asked.

"The post-office."

"Certainly they can. Your home is in the Soviet areas.[1]"

He guessed what was on my mind.

"Do you want to send a letter home?" he asked.

I nodded and said in a low voice, "I want to write a letter home, but. . . ."

"You still can't write it!" Chairman Mao completed my sentence for me. "Come, I'll write it for you."

I was overjoyed at this suggestion. On second thoughts I was ill at ease because I knew he was so busy and this would be taking up his precious time. But he went on encouragingly:

"What do you want to tell your father?" As he spoke he pushed the newspapers aside and took out some letter paper and a writing brush.

"I. . . ." What should I tell my father? I hadn't the slightest idea, so I said:

"Chairman Mao, you write what you think best. Anyway all I want to say is that things are fine in the Red Army. I feel all right with you. Very, very fine. That's all!"

He took down the address of my home and my father's name. Then I left to get the meal. When I came back with the food, Chairman Mao sat deep in thought, with his cheek cupped in one hand and a brush in the other. I knew it wasn't proper to ask him to eat at that moment, so I lightly placed the rice container on the table and went out.

---

[1] Liberated areas at that time were called Soviet areas

I lay myself down on the soft straw bed. I felt too overwhelmed with gratitude to sleep. I turned over from side to side, thinking of his kindness. I, the son of an ordinary peasant, had joined our own army and become the bodyguard of the Chairman of the Republic. (At that time I was no longer his orderly, but his bodyguard.) And now our Chairman Mao himself was writing a letter for me. In these past few years Chairman Mao had become like a father to me, concerning himself with my daily life and training. I would never forget this kind teacher. As I thought of these things tears trickled down my cheeks and dropped onto the straw pallet. The night was very still. I went out. A light shone in Chairman Mao's room. He was still working.

The next morning when I brought breakfast in, the Chairman gave me the letter he had written for me.

"Here's the letter. Will you see if it's all right?"

In great embarrassment, I put down the food container, took the letter with both hands and muttered, "Of course it'll be all right!"

"Go to the post-office and post it," the Chairman said.

"Your breakfast is ready," I reminded him.

"Leave it here. Go quickly!"

Instinctively I saluted him and left his office, hardly knowing what I was doing.

When I returned, the Chairman looked at me. "Now, do you feel relieved?" he said. "Still thinking of home?"

"No," I smiled. "I wouldn't go even if you ordered me!"

"What do you want to tell your father?" (p.13)

In the autumn of 1933, when our troops were attacking Chienchangfu, Chairman Mao and some other Central Committee members arrived in Kwangchang. This was quite near my home county, Ningtu, and suddenly the idea of going home popped up in my head. That very day I said to Chairman Mao:

"I know Kwangchang well. If I were to go back and visit my home, I'd know how to get there!"

Chairman Mao grinned. "Don't be in such a hurry. Easy does it! The further we go, the nearer we'll be to your home."

"Really?" I exclaimed. I was so glad that my heart leaped to my throat.

Two or three days later we arrived at the county that I had left so long ago. It was around two o'clock in the afternoon. Chairman Mao was staying with Comrade Li Fu-chun, then the Provincial Party Secretary of Kiangsi. When we had settled down, he sent for me and asked, "Want to go home?"

". . . Yes!"

"Good!" he replied. "I'll be attending several meetings these few days. You go home and take a look at things." He paused and looked at me quizzically: "How many days do you want?"

My head grew hot. I couldn't very well answer his question. Spreading his big hands, he asked: "Ten days? How's that?"

"Good," I said, and wanted to be off immediately. But just as I was about to go I suddenly thought: if I go, who will take care of his meals and drinking water? "No, Chairman. I'll not go!" I declared.

"What's up?" Chairman Mao looked at me curiously.

"If I go home, who'll prepare your meals?"

He smiled, and coming to me, put both hands on my shoulders, then said kindly, "Go and see your folks and then you'll work better when you come back. Your family is in the Soviet area now." He paused and then continued: "Don't come back here. Go straight to Changting and you'll find me there."

I nodded, but I was still reluctant to go. There was a conflict in my heart.

Then I was off on my way home in great excitement. Home . . . Chairman . . . Chairman . . . home. The rice fields were as beautiful as flowers under the setting sun. Home, my home was now in the Soviet area. Was there any place better than this? Then I thought of Chairman Mao. He was indeed a great leader of the poor people. Was there any man better than he?

It was already very dark when I arrived at the small stream where once I used to herd cattle. Lingnao, the village where I was born, could be seen on the opposite bank.

I got into the crowded ferry boat. My army uniform and the revolver I carried must have attracted the attention of the country folk who kept looking at me, whispering to one another.

"Excuse me," I spoke up, "do you know Chen Tai-hsiang (my father's name) in the village?"

For a moment all fell silent. I began to feel anxious. Then a voice came:

"Yes, there's a man called Chen Tai-hsiang."

"Oh, you are . . . !" a middle-aged man called me by my childhood name.

"Yes, yes, that's me!" I cried excitedly. Here was an old acquaintance. I would have jumped up if I had not been in a boat. As soon as the ice was broken the whole boat grew animated. Everybody was talking at once, all eager to tell me the news: how the village went Red, how the landlords and local despots were thrown down, how the land was distributed and my father had got his share. . . .

When we reached the opposite bank, the whole crowd accompanied me home. That evening there seemed to be a mass meeting at my house. All the village was there, including the chairman of the village Soviet. They asked me to tell them what it was like in the Red Army. As I spoke my father sat and smiled. It was the first time I had ever seen him smile so contentedly.

When they heard that I was Chairman Mao's bodyguard, they became still more interested and insisted I tell them more about our Chairman.

"Chairman Mao is just the same as we common folk," I said.

They were not satisfied with this and insisted that I tell them more about him. That night we talked until the cock crowed twice.

On the ninth day I set off for Changting to find Chairman Mao. On enquiry I was told that he was at the Central Hospital. I was worried. Was he sick? I rushed off to the hospital, but he was all right. There was no cause to worry.

He was glad to see me back. I gave him a present of peanuts and *tikua*[1] that my father had sent him. He accepted these gifts with a smile and asked, "How's your family?"

"Things are fine with them now!" I couldn't contain my excitement and poured out the story to him. "There's a Soviet in our village now; all the landlords and local despots have been beaten down. My family was given three rooms and sixteen *mu*[2] of land."

Chairman Mao nodded approval and said, "Good!" Then he asked, "Is the chairman of your village Soviet a rich man or a poor man?"

"A poor man who suffered just as my family suffered in the past!"

He wanted to know more about village affairs, and finally, half serious, half joking, asked: "Has your father found a mama for you?"

He had a good memory. It was when I had first met him over three years before that I had told him I had lost my mother.

"Yes. The neighbours told me it was a free choice marriage in new style." Chairman Mao chuckled with satisfaction.

---

[1] A kind of tuber crop

[2] A *mu* is equal to 1/6 acre.

First Step in
the Long March

A FTER presiding over a conference on financial and economic questions held in Shachoupa in the early summer of 1934, Chairman Mao went to the town of Wuyang in Juichin County, Kiangsi Province — then a model district for production in the central Soviet area — to undertake investigations into rural conditions. From there he went on to Huichang County, the seat of the Kwangtung-Kiangsi Provincial Party Committee, where he stayed for some time. Then he left for Yutu. In August he returned to Kaopinao near Juichin — the place where he was posted at that time. For several months, he was very busy, calling meetings of the responsible cadres in the localities he visited or making investigations in the villages.

The situation was becoming critical as the enemy launched the fifth encirclement campaign. Enemy planes roared overhead at all hours of the day, dropping bombs and strafing indiscriminately.

During those days, Chairman Mao was even busier. He lived in a big temple on a hillside together with Comrade Hsieh Chueh-tsai. In the daytime he walked about three *li* down the hill to attend meetings of the Military Council. When he came back he stayed up late writing. Many's the time he sent me down late at night to deliver the things he had written to Vice-Chairman Chou En-lai and other leaders. I did not know what these manuscripts were until later when they appeared as booklets printed on red and green paper. They were on questions of tactics in guerrilla warfare.

Every day many people came up the hill to where we lived. The Chairman was not too well. Often he ate nothing and slept little. He lost a great deal of weight, and we bodyguards became worried. But what could we do? Every time we suggested that he should take a rest, he would point at the pile of documents on his desk and say, as though he were consulting with us: "I'll take a rest as soon as I've finished these. Will that be all right?" There was, however, no end to these documents which came in a constant stream. We began to think of getting a doctor for him.

One evening after dinner, when the Chairman was standing on the steps in front of the temple, deep in thought, Director Yuan Fu-ching of the General Affairs Office and a leading comrade of the Central Hospital arrived. I was overjoyed to see them as I was sure that their visit had to do with getting a doctor for the Chairman. As I understood it, anyone who was sick, whoever he might be, must obey doctor's orders.

After they had shaken hands, they began to talk. I stood aside getting ready — if occasion allowed — to put in a word or two to secure a good doctor for the Chairman.

Director Yuan first raised the subject of getting a groom. What about a doctor? I was becoming impatient. It was only after a long talk that Yuan said:

"Chairman, we've found a good doctor for you. He'll go along with you."

I almost jumped. Now something was happening! "Fine!" I burst out. "Send him to the Chairman quickly!"

Then I remembered that I should not have spoken this way in the presence of superiors, and I felt embarrassed.

The Chairman looked at me and then at Director Yuan and his companion. Lighting a cigarette, he began slowly: "I don't think a doctor is necessary. A nurse will do — it's just taking temperatures and giving injections. . . ."

"Chairman," Yuan did not wait for him to finish, "judging by your present condition, I think it's better to have a doctor, and we've already. . . ."

"No," interrupted Chairman Mao. "The army needs doctors. We've very few of them. How can I keep a doctor all for myself?" Then he smiled, "My health's not bad. Won't a nurse do just as well?"

Director Yuan and the other comrade wanted to say something more. But knowing the Chairman's nature, they did not insist. They left soon afterwards.

A few days later, a young man about eighteen carrying a knapsack marked with a red cross came to us. He was Chung Fu-chang, the medical orderly who was to accompany the Chairman all through the Long March.

About that time, we received orders from Chairman Mao to equip ourselves lightly in preparation to go to the front (we did not know that this was going to be the Long March to northern Shensi). We bodyguards felt it rather odd. Why was the order for light equipment so strict this time? Even the Chairman did not take his nine-compartment knapsack with him. His entire equipment consisted of two blankets, a cotton sheet, an oilcloth, a worn overcoat, a broken umbrella and a bundle of books.

"We're going to the front to fight!" This was the theme of animated discussion on all sides.

At the end of September we left Kaopinao for Yutu with Chairman Mao.

October 18, 1934 was an unforgettable date in the history of the Chinese revolution. At a little after five that afternoon, some twenty of us left Yutu in the company of Chairman Mao. It was the first step on the Long March.

Passing the northern gate of Yutu in a westerly direction, we came to a broad river along which we made our way upstream. The muddy water foamed and roared. Sunset brought cold breezes. The Chairman wore no overcoat. He was wearing only his grey uniform and Red Army cap. Taking the lead he strode firmly ahead.

When we reached a point 20 *li* from Yutu, we heard shouting and saw the gleam of lights in the distance.

Medical orderly Chung Fu-chang and I were at a loss to know what to make of it.

"They're our troops," said Chairman Mao.

Our troops? I thought. We hadn't seen a single soldier when we left Yutu. How could there be so many in this place all of a sudden? I was puzzled.

As we neared the shore, we found large numbers of Red troops on both sides of the river. The whole place was in a hubbub, with thousands of torches moving to and fro, and singing, laughing and shouting from one end to the other. Pontoons were thrown across the wide river to make a bridge and the troops were marching across in a continuous stream.

I was delighted and rushed up to the Chairman. "How's it that we've so many troops?" I asked in a loud voice. He smiled. "That's not all," he said quietly. "Many more have gone on ahead of these!"

We followed Chairman Mao onto the pontoon. A great throng of soldiers on horseback, on foot, carriers and country folk sending the troops off were moving across in a steady stream. The Chairman stopped now and then to make way for others.

At about midnight we met a stretcher carrying a wounded soldier coming in the opposite direction. The country folk on the road were in great excitement.

"Kupi and Hsintien will soon be captured!" they told us.

Chairman Mao walked up to the stretcher and pulled the coverlet up a little to cover the wounded man. "Is your wound very bad, comrade?" he asked gently.

The man on the stretcher stared at Chairman Mao under the light of a torch. He was obviously moved. "No, not too bad!" he replied. "I'll be back at the front very soon!"

As the stretcher passed on, the Chairman stood gazing after it, absorbed in thought.

Just before daybreak, a party of country folk crossed our path, almost every one of them carrying a heavy sack.

"Where are you from?" I went up to ask them.

"Kupi and Hsintien have been captured!" they spoke in one voice.

"What have you got there?"

"Salt! It's as precious as gold!"

They were guides from the old Soviet area and they were carrying back salt from Kupi and Hsintien. There was a crying need for salt in the Soviet area just then.

Chairman Mao waved to them. "This time you won't have to worry over salt, eh?" he said.

At dawn, crowds of people appeared on the road, surging back and forth. On the walls, on the trees and everywhere in the villages posters announced the news of our victory: "Our troops have captured Kupi and Hsintien!" and "Celebrate our first great victory!"

"Is your wound very bad, comrade?" (p.25)

Passing the Miao Region

HAVING broken through the enemy's fourth blockade line — the Hsiang River, the Red Army reached a main road on the border of Kwangsi and Hunan in November 1934. It was pitch-dark when our little party arrived there, as we had travelled mostly at night to avoid being discovered by enemy planes. At dawn we found ourselves in a tiny mountain village.

We had been marching and fighting all the way. Chairman Mao had not had a single square meal. As soon as the troops took a rest, Comrade Tseng Hsien-chi, a fellow-bodyguard, and I went to look for something to eat. It was a small village and the inhabitants were very poor. The only thing we were able to buy was some 20 catties of *tikua*. I had them cooked and brought in to the Chairman. He was sitting on a small stool, chatting with the body-guards and groom around him. "The crossing of the Hsiang River was a very great success!" he was saying.

Indeed, our crossing of the Hsiang River the previous night had been no mean feat.

Tseng Hsien-chi and I, holding the earthen pots, announced that dinner was ready. We went up to Chairman Mao and asked him to have his meal. Taking a *tikua*, he began to eat. Then he said:

"We'll soon reach the region inhabited by the Miao people!"

The Miao region! This was something new. I remembered a teacher at some classes on political study once telling us that the Miao people were a national minority, rather backward in their culture and economy, that their customs and ways were quite different from ours, and that they were even more ruthlessly persecuted by the White Army.[1] But what they looked like remained something of a mystery.

"They are like us, the Han people," the Chairman went on. "They also want to carry on a revolutionary movement against the oppression of the White Army. So they are our good brothers."

Chairman Mao told us in great detail about the oppression of the Miao people at the hands of the White Army, their customs, habits, religious beliefs, and so on. He called on us to keep to our rules of work among the masses even more strictly once we had entered the Miao region. He cautioned us against wandering about and tampering with things that didn't belong to us. He told us that the Miao women were also different from the

---

[1] The Kuomintang and warlord armies

women in the Soviet area, who treated the Red soldiers as brothers and, indeed, addressed them as such. The Miao women were not used to this kind of relationship. They still had feudal ideas.

Listening to the Chairman's talk, we felt in something of a dilemma. Was this a "forbidden zone" we were going into? How were we going to get on when we put up our tents and needed to borrow things? I asked Chairman Mao if it would be all right to take down a door board[1] for him to sleep on, as we usually did wherever we stopped for the night.

"No, it won't do!" he said firmly. Then smiling he asked, "Didn't I warn you not to take things that do not belong to us?"

"What will you sleep on, then?"

"Anything will do except their doors!"

I was a bit downcast and had nothing more to say. The Miao people must be very different from us Hans, I thought to myself. They must be a very rough lot. Just then, someone started to snore. It was Huang Ying-ho, the carrier. He had fallen asleep beside the Chairman, holding the remains of the *tikua* in his hand.

Chairman Mao was amused. "That's all right," he said. "It's what we should all do after a hearty meal. Tonight we've to march on."

Though I needed sleep badly, I lay awake. All the others were awake, too, except Huang Ying-ho. As dawn turned

---

[1] It was the custom of the peasants to allow the Red Army to take down their door boards to use as beds, and put them back again next morning

into morning, enemy planes came roaring their messages of death and dropping bombs from time to time, destroying people's homes and uprooting the rice in the fields.

That same evening we resumed our march. The November nights were bitterly cold and there was no moon.

All through the night, we trekked over the mountains, going up hill one moment and down dale the next. Sometimes we clambered up steep slopes and slid down the other side. When we reached the top of a peak, the sky seemed to be right over us. Then the Chairman would look around and make sure everyone was there before going ahead again.

The next dawn found us coming down a mountain. Opposite us on the side of a small mountain were some strange-looking wooden houses of a type we had never seen before. They were neither one-storied nor two-storied, but like baskets hung in the air. Chairman Mao told us that we were in the Miao region.

The sun was rising when we reached the mountain village. With the morning mist thinning out, we could see the houses more clearly. The mountain formed their back walls, so they were, actually, an extension of the slopes. Under them were the pigsties or sheepfolds. A tiny stream ran down from the mountain, forming a small pond here and there as it passed below the windows.

The windows of the house in which the Chairman stayed gave onto a large pond with many big-headed carp.

"Let's get some fish for the Chairman," suggested Wu Chieh-ching, one of the Chairman's bodyguards. Of course, this was a bright idea. But how could we dare, after what Chairman had told us the day before?

We all remained silent.

"After all, the owner of this house may be a local despot," Wu Chieh-ching pressed his point.

"I think p'raps we'd better ask the Chairman first," said Huang Ying-ho slowly.

When I took some water into Chairman Mao's room, I found him about to take a rest. I put the water on a bamboo table, and stood for a while, wondering how to begin.

"Chairman," I found a way out at last, "are you hungry?"

"Is there anything to eat?"

"Oh, yes!" I said quickly.

"What is there?" the Chairman turned to look at me.

I poured out some water, and said as casually as I could, "Fish, some big fish!"

"Where are you going to get them from?" the Chairman asked.

"Right here!" I pointed at the pond outside the window.

The Chairman walked to the window and looked. Then he turned to me. "Have you forgotten so quickly what I told you yesterday?" he said sternly.

I hung my head and said softly, "We'll pay money."

"That won't do either."

"Just buy a few," I insisted.

The Chairman came and sat down beside me, and patiently explained the characteristics of the national minorities and our policy towards them. "No matter how big their sheep or fish are, you should not touch them," he said. "They may be keeping them to use as sacrifices to their gods."

Then he finished up by telling me to explain to all the others that we should never tamper with the things belonging to these people, not even we paid money to buy them.

I said I would, and came out. Wu Chieh-ching was apparently waiting for news from me outside, for I ran straight into him. Immediately he asked what was the result.

"The Chairman doesn't approve!" I said bluntly.

"We'll pay money!"

"Not even we pay money!" I shouted into his ear. "This is discipline, understand?" Then I was off.

In the afternoon, a party of about a dozen men turned up, dressed in Han clothes and carrying rifles. They asked to see the Chairman.

Hastily buttoning up my jacket, I asked them where they were from.

They were very well-mannered — contrary to what I had expected. One of them spoke up. "We are local people!" he said in the Kwangsi dialect. His accent was difficult to understand.

Local people? I thought. Then they must be Miaos. What do they want to see the Chairman for — and carrying rifles?

"Have you a letter of introduction?" I asked them.

"Yes, yes," a big fellow pulled a small piece of paper out of his pocket.

I took it to the Chairman.   He was studying a map.
"Chairman, there's somebody to see you."   I reported.

"Who is it?" asked he.

"Some local people," I handed over the piece of paper.
"They're carrying rifles!"

Having read what was on the piece of paper, the Chairman turned to me, delight written all over his face.   "Ask
them to come in at once."   Then he walked out to meet
his guests.

I accompanied the strangers into the Chairman's room
and retired.   I was a bit puzzled.   What was their
business?   Why was the Chairman so friendly to them?

The strangers remained in the Chairman's room for a
long time.   It was nearly sunset when they left.

When I brought dinner in, the Chairman was still standing before the map which was now covered with red circles.
"Will you take your dinner, Chairman?"   I said, putting
the dishes down quietly.

He turned and laid down his pencil.   "You haven't
taken other people's fish, have you?" he asked with a smile.

I smiled back and shook my head.

"Chairman," I asked, "what do these people do?"

"They're Miao comrades!" he said elatedly.

"The Miao people also have rifles?"   I was curious.

The Chairman glanced at me.   "They are Miao
guerrillas — our comrades!" he said.

"We have comrades among the Miao people?"   I
exclaimed.

"We have comrades everywhere and there are Communists everywhere!"   Then his eyes twinkled.   "Do you

think we monopolize the revolution?" he said humorously. I smiled.

The same evening we resumed our journey. I told Wu Chieh-ching privately, "Do you know that there are Communists and guerrillas — our comrades — among the Miao people?"

"Really?" Wu was skeptical.

New Year
by the Wu River

IT was the last day of 1934 when the Central Red Army reached Houchang near Huangping County, Kweichow Province. We were to camp here over the year's end.

Houchang was a town where country fairs were held. It had a busy market. It was the largest place we had come to since leaving Juichin.

As soon as we arrived, Chairman Mao went to a meeting at the headquarters of the Military Council. According to our bodyguard rota, Tseng Hsien-chi and I were on the first shift that day to accompany the Chairman to the meeting, while Chueh Kuei-lan and Lin Yutsai were to look out for living quarters for him.

Before sunset, Chueh came to relieve me so that I could go and get something to eat. He told me to come back quickly so that I could take the Chairman home early.

"Have you got everything shipshape?" I asked.

"You go there and see," he winked at me, looking mysterious.

I came to the troops' camping ground. It looked quite different to any of our earlier camps. Everyone was in high spirits. Some soldiers in thin army uniform were sweeping snow on the streets, others were carrying door boards to put up beds, still others were practising songs. I learned that we were preparing to pass the New Year's Eve and there was going to be a New Year party in the evening with a variety of entertainments. I was tremendously excited. The fatigue of our several days' march vanished with the snowflakes. I quickened my steps, dragging fellow-bodyguard Tseng Hsien-chi by the hand. "Let's go to see how they've fixed things. As soon as the Chairman comes back, we'll see in the New Year and have some fun!" I said.

The house provided for the Chairman was of Peking style, with rooms on four sides and a large courtyard in the centre. Two big imposing snow-men stood facing the gate. The brick path across the courtyard was as clean as if it had just been washed. The three spacious and bright rooms facing south were to be the Chairman's living quarters. The one in the middle was to be the sitting room. A kerosene lamp was hung from the ceiling. Against one wall was a long narrow tea table — antique style. In front of this was a large square table with heavy arm-chairs on two sides. On the wall facing the entrance was a large painting of a laughing arhat, hands folded on the chest. as if in welcome. The room on the left was to be the Chairman's bedroom. One glance at it told us that Chueh and Lin had taken great pains in arranging everything. They had put so much straw on the bed that it was as soft as any sofa could be. The room on the right was to be the Chairman's office. Two tables placed together made a desk on which were stationery and telephone. "Beautiful!" Tseng Hsien-chi and I exclaimed in delight as we walked round the room. Never before had the Chairman had such a good house to live in, not even in the old Soviet area, let alone during the Long March. What a treat it was to know that he would have such a fine place as this to rest up in! It meant more to us bodyguards than anything else, especially for New Year's Eve.

Something was still wanting in these rooms. Yes, the stools! Let's get them quickly! Tseng and I rushed out and returned with some thirty square wooden stools which we placed round the desk as if a banquet were going to begin. Tseng wanted to know why we needed so many seats. I told him that since this was New Year's Eve, the Central Committee members and the leading comrades from general headquarters would certainly come to join the Chairman for the New Year celebrations. What would they do if there was nothing to sit on?

Tseng Hsien-chi kept nodding as he listened.

Then I consulted him about what food we should prepare for the Chairman. "Well, this is New Year," he said. "We should prepare the things he likes best." So I recited a list of the Chairman's favourites: beef, chilli, fried bean-curd. . . .

"And don't forget sweet, fermented rice!" Tseng shouted at the top of his voice as if he had hit on a wonderful idea.

It was already dark when we had everything prepared. Tseng and I went to meet the Chairman, carrying a lamp with us.

We found that the meeting was still going on. Chueh Kuei-lan looked very pleased with himself. "Well," he said, "are you satisfied, comrades?" Now I knew why he had acted so mysteriously. He had wanted to give us a surprise. I held out my fist, thumb upwards, to indicate my admiration and he gave me a satisfied smile.

It was ten o'clock before the meeting was over. As the Chairman was putting on his overcoat, I went up to meet him with the lamp. We had walked a little way when he asked us how far it was to the place where he was to spend the night. I answered that it was about two or three *li* away.

It was snowing and the wind was sharp. The clothes the Chairman had on were not warm enough. As I walked behind him, lamp in hand, a sudden emotion seized me. It was over two months since we had left the Soviet area, and the Chairman had been so busy that he had hardly had any time for rest. During the march, he would often give his horse to the weak or sick comrades while he himself would walk. While in camp, he attended meetings, and would be reading telegrams, drafting documents, and so on when most of the others had gone to sleep. How could he keep on like this? How splendid it would be if he could stay in a nice place

like this for a few more days, pass the New Year pleasant-
ly and enjoy a good rest!

I could not bottle it up any longer. "Chairman," I said,
"this is New Year. We should take a good rest here.
We've prepared everything!"

The Chairman halted. He turned and faced me,
straightening my cap and speaking very gently: "What?
You have arranged everything to pass the New Year?"

"Yes, everything's been arranged!" said Tseng Hsien-
chi.

The Chairman looked at me, then at Tseng. He said
nothing. He seemed absorbed in thought.

What was the matter? Perhaps he had not heard what
we'd said. He might still be thinking of the questions
discussed at the meeting.

After a long suspense, the Chairman spoke, "We can't
stay here; we've much more important things to do than
pass the time of the New Year!"

"What is it we have to do?" I was puzzled.

"We've to race against time to cross the barrier of the
Wu River," the Chairman began, stopping to pat us on
the shoulder. "We're the Red Army. What's the most
important thing for the Red Army to do at present? To
fight the enemy. To cross the Wu River is very important.
You think Houchang is a big place. No. There are many
big places in China, much bigger than this one. Tsunyi
for instance. And there are still bigger ones than Tsunyi.
When we've crossed the Wu River and taken Tsunyi, it'll
be more interesting to spend the New Year then and
there."

He told us briefly about the general situation. Chiang Kai-shek was sending several detachments under Hsueh Yo and Chou Hun-yuan to follow us closely. We must get across the Wu River as fast as possible to avoid contact with the enemy.

It is difficult to describe my feelings when I heard what the Chairman had to say. Nevertheless, the idea of racing across the Wu River was a stimulating one and my excitement began to mount.

Arriving at the house, we found it brilliantly lighted by the big lamp in the centre room. The Chairman smiled at us. "It's really like New Year!" So saying, he took out some documents and settled down to work up late. He told us that he had had his dinner at headquarters and that we needn't prepare anything for him.

"But we have something good for you!" Tseng was quick to say.

"What do you have?" he raised his head.

"Sweet fermented rice, your favourite!"

"Very well," said the Chairman, standing up and waving his hand towards the circle of stools, "let's spend the New Year's Eve together here!"

After taking some food, he told us to go to bed while he went on with his work.

About four o'clock next morning, information came that our vanguard unit had reached the Wu River, whereupon we set out in the same direction.

On the Bank of
the Golden Sand River

IT was on an evening in April 1935, I remember, that the 9th, 1st and 5th Red Army Corps — all belonging to the First Front Red Army (the Central Red Army) — and the Central Committee staff reached the Golden Sand River. The Golden Sand River was the first big river to face us after the crossing of the Wu River. It was in spate, with angry dragon-headed waves confronting us. All the leading comrades were taken up with the problem of crossing, as we had only a few boats at our command. Chairman Mao, of course, was in the thick of these discussions.

Just before dawn I crossed with him in a boat. We had hardly landed when he was off with Comrade Liu Po-cheng, the Chief of Staff, to plan the next stage of the march. I set about looking for somewhere for him to use as a temporary office and living quarters.

It didn't look hopeful. The river bank was nothing but bare rocks, with a few holes in the cliffs, dripping with moisture, hardly big enough to be called caves. I sought in vain for planks or even straw to use for a bed. In the end I had to lay out a piece of oilcloth on the ground and put the blanket on it, feeling that that would at least give him something to lie down on — he hadn't rested at all the whole night. Come to that, he'd had no rest for the last few days.

My next task was to lay out his documents, maps and papers. Usually I did it with his secretary, Comrade Huang Yu-feng, whenever we made camp. We used to rig up some kind of a table or desk. But now there was nothing at all to use even as a makeshift, and Comrade Huang was still on the other side of the river. How could the Chairman do his work? I tried pinning one map up on the wall of the cave, but it was no good — it was just sand and wouldn't hold the nail, and there wasn't room to spread the documents out. Already I had wasted enough time; I was expecting Chairman Mao back from his conference any minute, and I hadn't even got a drop of boiled water ready. I knew he would need it, after his night's work. I put aside the problem of finding a desk and hurried out to see what I could do about the water.

It was broad daylight when Chairman Mao came back and sent for me. When I reached the cave I saw him standing there, deep in thought.

"You've come back," I said.

"M'm . . . everything ready?"

"I've done what I can," I said, pointing at the "bed". "There are no boards to be found, so I've made this up. Will you lie down for a bit? The water will be boiled any minute."

I turned to go to see how the water was getting on, but he called me back.

"Haven't you found me a place to work?" he asked.

"Comrade Huang hasn't come over yet," I said without thinking. "I couldn't find anything to use as a desk — not even a small table. Will you have some water first?"

He took a step towards me, as though he had not heard what I told him, and said, very seriously, but not at all angrily, "The work's the all-important thing at a moment like this. Food, or drink are trifles. Twenty to thirty thousand of our comrades are still waiting to cross the river there. It's a matter of thirty thousand lives!"

I didn't know what to say, but stood there gazing at him. I could feel my heart pounding. He came right up to me. "Go on," he said. "Find me a board or something to use as a desk before you do anything else."

I pulled myself together and ran off, and by hunting high and low found a small board which must have been used as a door for a cave mouth. Chairman Mao helped me set it up, spreading out his maps and documents. Then I remembered the water; it must have boiled by now. I got up to fetch it, when the Chairman spoke to me again.

"Chen Chang-feng!"

"Yes?"

"Come back!"

I went back right into the cave, standing before the "desk".

"I'll have to give you some punishment, you know," he said. Although the tone of his voice was mild as usual, I felt the air very tense. I realized how I had failed in my job, and stood looking at him, very miserable.

"I want you to stay by me and keep awake."

I felt an uneasy smile come over my face and sat down opposite him.

"Right," I said.

He had got telegrams and documents all over the desk. The field telephone was transmitting messages all the time, and he was absolutely immersed in work. He had not allowed a minute for his own comfort. I found it hard to keep the tears back as I realized that I had wasted his time over the desk, and if I had understood my job, I would have had it ready before.

I was awfully drowsy, and had a habit anyway of dropping off beside him when he was working. I knew what he meant when he said he would "punish" me by asking me to keep awake, although he had spoken half in jest. But that day when I saw him heart and soul in his work, I had not the least desire to sleep. From time to time he looked at me with a cheerful smile. I felt terribly uneasy. I got up and fetched the boiled water, and poured some out to cool.

Time enough to eat two meals passed before Chairman Mao stopped and stood up to stretch himself.

"You've been with me several years now," he said. "How is it that you still don't understand what comes first? The first thing you have to do when we make a stop is to find some place for me to work. Food and rest are quite secondary to that. You must realize that to us work is and will be the most important thing under all circumstances." He stopped a minute and then rubbed his hand over my head. "Now go and get some sleep," he said. "You can hardly keep your eyes open."

After what the Chairman had just said, of course I didn't want to go. He urged me again. I was nearly in tears — I couldn't help it. It wasn't because I had been criticized. It was a mixed feeling of regret and joy, the sort of feeling you have when you have done something wrong and your parents speak seriously but not harshly to you in warning: "My child, don't do it again! Now go and play!"

For three days and nights while some 30,000 troops continued crossing the Golden Sand River, Chairman Mao never left his "desk".

The Yi People Welcome Chairman Mao

SOON after the crossing we reached Mienning in southeast Sikang. There we received orders to get ready to enter the region inhabited by the Yi people, and to cross the Tatu River. Each of us was required to carry enough rations for fourteen days, a bamboo pole, and a seven-metre-long rope. In the streets we could see people transporting grain and bamboo poles, and plaiting ropes with all available materials.

One day we were chatting with our host. He was a very talkative old chap and once he got going it was difficult to stop him. He could turn a molehill into a mountain at a moment's notice. When the conversation turned to the Yi people he suddenly became very agitated and cried in alarm: "That's the Lolos, eh? Ah, they're fierce, they are!"

"How fierce?" we asked him, and he carried on in great excitement: "They're savages and love to fight! They specially hate us Han people. They see red as soon as they catch sight of a Han, and if they catch you — well, it's all up with you!"

"If they're that fierce, we'd better keep out of their way!" said Tseng Hsien-chi.

"How can you keep away from them unless you keep away from their territory?" retorted our host. "Once in there, you'll land yourselves in a trap. Suddenly you'll find a whole mountain full of their men, yelling and shouting, and sniping at you. It's said they're first-rate shots!"

"Why do they hate the Hans so much?" we asked.

The old man frowned and shook his head. "I don't know!" he said.

Although we didn't quite believe all he told us about the Yis, we were a bit worried. Particularly about the sniping. We were puzzled too because in our political study class we had often discussed this question of the national minorities. We knew that the White Army oppressed them worse than it did the Hans, so we looked on them as our brothers. We'd not heard anything about them killing Hans, so I went and asked Chairman Mao.

"Chairman, it's said the Yis are very fierce!" I began.

"Who told you that?" he rejoined. So I told him all that our host had said and asked him: "Is it true?"

Chairman Mao smiled and countered: "What do you think?"

I smiled in my turn and shook my head.

He then explained that the Yis in Szechuan and the Miaos in Kwangsi were cruelly oppressed by the White Army. This was why they hated the Whites. "But to us," he said, "they're different. We respect them and look on them as our brothers. We unite with them and fight together with them against oppression by the White Army. The Yis will be glad when they know that the Red Army has come to them. So what's there to be afraid of?"

"But that old man spoke as if what he said was truth itself!"

Chairman Mao explained: "Those are simply rumours deliberately spread by the White Army to stir up hatred between Hans and Yis. That old man hasn't seen things with his own eyes, so naturally it's easy to deceive him."

Chairman Mao's explanations set our minds at rest.

Two days later we left Mienning. We reached the Yi region at noon. It was May. In my native Kiangsi, the fields would already be gay with the golden rice, but here the land was deserted and untilled. There were no rice fields, no farm houses, only some rough low shacks in the forests.

But soon after we entered a mountainous area a group of men and women in strange clothes suddenly appeared before us. They shouted as they approached. I and Tseng Hsien-chi were frankly alarmed. It was only when they came near to us that I saw clearly that they came not to fight but to welcome us. Five tall women came out from the group, each carrying a big red cock in her arms. They approached Chairman Mao and surrounded him. They

They approached Chairman Mao and surrounded him. (p.31)

said something that we could not understand. But Chairman Mao nodded his head and imitating their gestures, put his hands before his breast to show his gratitude. I, Tseng Hsien-chi and other comrades imitated him in turn to thank them.

Then Chairman Mao, closely followed by the women with the cocks, walked on. By this time there were Yi people everywhere, on the slopes, in the valley, and on the top of the mountain. Some of them raised their hands high in welcome, some bowed, others sang gaily. It was a strange and moving sight that brought tears to our eyes.

Chairman Mao turned to us: "See! All that talk about fighting. They've come to welcome us! Just think why!" As we walked on, we discussed the matter.

A while later Tseng asked: "Chairman, although they are our good brothers, we can't understand what they say. It's as if we were in a foreign country!"

"It's not surprising," Chairman Mao said. "You know how big our country is. You, a Kiangsi man, can't even understand what I, a Hunan man, say. So how can you understand what the Yi people say?"

This set all of us laughing. When the Yi people saw us laughing, they too laughed, uproariously. The way they laughed was so simple and unaffected that one wondered at that wicked talk about their fierceness and cruelty. And it was in this atmosphere, full of gaiety and friendship, that we crossed the "mysterious" Yi region.

From Anshunchang to the Luting Bridge

AFTER leaving the mountains of the Yi people we marched about 200 *li* with Chairman Mao until we came to Anshunchang on the Tatu River. From there, we continued north along the bank. We heard we would pass through a market town called Mohsimien and proceed to Luting where we would cross a bridge to the other side.

It was a mountainous region, a trackless wilderness of heavy grass and stiff brush. Though Chairman Mao had a horse (which he seldom rode even where the road was not rough, but would offer to the wounded or weak comrades), it was useless, and he walked along with us.

The higher we climbed up the steep path, the tougher the going became and the denser grew the vegetation. From time to time we had to stop to let the engineer units hack a trail through.

But regardless of the road, Chairman Mao walked briskly. His face showed not the slightest trace of fatigue, though we had been marching and fighting and working hard for a long time. He frequently turned around to talk with us or tell us stories.

Seeing the Chairman like this, we perked up. Our weariness vanished into the clouds.

At dusk we reached a mountain top. Anshunchang was far behind. The unit travelling with us stopped to rest. I talked it over with Tseng Hsien-chi and the others, then walked up to the Chairman and asked, "Shall we rest too?"

The Chairman halted and looked at me. "Tired?"

"Oh, no. But you see, they've started cooking."

"Ah." The Chairman laughed. "Tell the others that we'll rest and eat too."

When they saw that the Chairman had stopped, the bodyguards, porters and grooms all gathered around. We sat down beside a stream and ate our dry rations. The Chairman ate with us.

"It would be better for us to get some water to drink," a young comrade cried. His mentioning of water made us more thirsty. All of us wanted a drink.

The Chairman looked at us, smiling. "A lot of water here," he pointed at the flowing stream. He scooped up the water with his hands and took a big mouthful, saying, "Good. Very cool and sweet." We all bent down to have a good drink.

Suddenly we heard snoring. We didn't have to look to know it was Huang. He certainly fell asleep quickly.

We grinned. Wu Chieh-ching couldn't resist. He scooped some water from the stream and tiptoed over to Huang.

"He's worn out, let him rest awhile." At the sound of the voice we turned to see the Chairman. He stooped down beside Huang, gently raised his head from the grassy tussock, and slipped his own folded tunic under for a pillow. Huang stirred, smiled faintly and sank back into slumber.

We stood and watched, entranced. The Chairman turned to us and smiled. "You get some rest, too. We've more marching to do tomorrow."

Without a word, we bedded down right there. I stretched out on a flat rock.

Dusk is cool in early summer. Though I was very tired, I couldn't fall asleep. Huang was sound asleep on the Chairman's tunic. The Chairman was pacing the mountain top, obviously deep in thought. I could hear the roaring of the Tatu River far below us. The last light of the setting sun turned the entire sky red, and changed Chairman Mao's uniform from grey to orange.

That night the Chairman slept with us on the mountain.

The next day we set out early in the morning. As we neared Mohsimien we came to a broad, deep river. We couldn't wade across, and the only bridge was a mere two metres wide.

Troops were already crossing when we got there and it was crowded with men. When they saw the Chairman, they immediately cleared a way for him.

Before the Chairman could say anything, the groom led his horse onto the bridge. As it set foot on the rickety structure, the animal shied and whinnied in terror, adding to the general confusion.

The Chairman hurried to the bridge. "Don't take him over yet," he called to the groom. "Let the comrades cross first."

"He's carrying your clothes and luggage," the groom shouted back.

We knew that was the case. Unless the horse was taken over, the Chairman would have no bedding that night. So we chimed in with the groom by saying, "Let them lead him over gradually, Chairman."

"It will be awkward if we don't get him across."

The Chairman gave us a kindly and yet reproving glance. "Help the groom bring that horse back, Chen Chang-feng," he said. "Let the troops pass first."

The soldiers had been aiding the groom coax the horse along. I had to run to the middle of the bridge to bring the animal back.

When we returned him to the bank, the Chairman urged the soldiers to cross over quickly. Only when the last of them had reached the opposite shore did we follow the Chairman across.

That night we reached Mohsimien. The Chairman said to us, "Remember, we must think of our troops, think of others, no matter where or when. If we held up the march of all those comrades just for the sake of our single horse, that would be pretty bad, wouldn't it?"

After leaving there, we went with the Chairman to Luting. The river was narrower than at Anshunchang, but the current was swifter, and both sides were lined with cliffs.

The bridge consisted of thirteen thick steel chains fixed to big iron spikes driven into the rock at either end. Chains running along each side of the bridge served as railings.

At Luting we met Comrade Liu Ya-lou and other leaders. They took the Chairman to a place in front of a large church, where they took a good view of the surroundings. Then we went with the Chairman to the bridge.

Originally, there had been planks spread across the cables. The enemy had set fire to them and destroyed them before our advance unit captured the bridge. I walked up and looked at those cables, each as thick as a bowl, at the charred planks and the seething river below. I felt nervous.

The Chairman noticed this. He pointed his finger at me and asked, "Scared?"

"No."

He started across, with all of us right behind. I watched him carefully. He walked so lightly, so naturally. He looked up at the cliffs towering into the clouds on either shore. The roaring of the water was unable to disrupt his thoughts. Because there were so many people on the bridge, when we reached the middle it began to sway. I grabbed the chain railing and stopped. The Chairman turned his head and said something to me. But I couldn't hear a thing. The thunder of the river obliterated all other sound. Obviously he was asking whether I was having trouble. I shook my head. He halted and took my hand. Then we walked on together.

I stared downward for a moment. Huge boiling waves seemed to thrust up like long swords stabbing at the bridge. It made me dizzy. I raised my eyes and looked at my comrades on the bridge. Some were advancing cautiously step by step, some were crawling prone along the steel cables. Others were walking in a line, hand in hand, chatting and laughing.

Still leading me by the hand, the Chairman kept looking back at the men following. Sometimes he stopped and waved at them, or said a few words. At last we left the bridge behind us.

"Chairman," I said when we reached the shore, "with one squad we could hold a bridge like that indefinitely. But the enemy. . . ."

The Chairman laughed. "The enemy are the enemy. We can't compare them with an army led by our Communist Party. Right?"

"Right!" we chorused.

On the Road to Shuitseti

WE stayed a few days in Hualingping after crossing the Tatu River. Then we set out for Shuitseti. People said we could reach it in a day's march.

We started in the morning. Chairman Mao was busy, so he didn't go with the Central Committee organizations but travelled instead with the medical units, which left later. Comrade Hu Chang-pao, leader of the guard squad, and I went with him.

When we came to a mountain which was about six *li* to the summit, three enemy planes started diving towards us. We spread out but continued marching. Hu was walking ahead of the Chairman, I behind. The Chairman marched with his eyes on the road, as if pondering some question. Only occasionally did he look up at the planes. The rest of us were very tense.

The planes swung around and went off in the direction from which we had come. Just as we were feeling a bit relieved, from above and behind us we heard two piercing whistles. I knew at once they were bombs.

"Chairman," I yelled, rushing towards him.

I had run only a few steps when a cluster of bombs exploded ahead and to one side of me. The blast knocked me down. The Chairman was engulfed in smoke. I crawled to my feet and looked towards the Chairman. He was squatting beside Hu Chang-pao, who had been hit. The Chairman hadn't been hurt. My heart, which had been in my mouth, settled back into its normal place. I automatically wiped the sweat and dust from my brow and ran over to the Chairman. He was stroking Hu's head. Hu was lying with his hands pressed against his belly. Big beads of sweat stood out on his forehead. But he wasn't uttering a sound.

I didn't know what to do. The medical orderly came hurrying towards us.

"Quick," the Chairman urged him, "take care of him."

Hu waved his hand in refusal. "Chairman, I'm finished," he said. "Keep the medicine. The rest of you still have to go on." His ruddy face had become a waxy yellow.

"It's not serious. You'll be all right," the Chairman said comfortingly. He swiftly helped the medical orderly bind Hu's wounds. Then he sat down and cradled Hu in his arms like a sleepy child. "You'll be all right. Hang on a little longer," he said softly. "We'll carry you to Shuitseti. We'll find a doctor and have you back in shape in no time."

Hu gazed up fondly at the Chairman with dimming eyes. But he became quite upset when he heard that we were going to carry him. Labouring to get the words out, he said, "Chairman, it's no use. The blood's all flowing into my stomach. I don't mind dying. My only regret is that I can't go with you to northern Shensi and see our base there." Two glistening tears rolled from the corners of his eyes. He gasped for a while as if he felt a lump in his throat, then added, "My parents live in Chian, Kiangsi. Please tell them of my death, if possible."

The Chairman didn't say anything, but only held him closer.

"You'll get well," the medical orderly and I said encouragingly. "You'll go with us to northern Shensi."

Hu shook his head. "Comrade Chen," he said to me, his words coming slowly, "I can no longer protect the Chairman. You must guard him and the other Central Committee leaders well."

His voice was so low I could barely hear him. Finally, with a great effort, he raised his head and stared fixedly at the Chairman and us. His lips trembled as he forced out the words, "Victory . . . to . . . the . . . revolution!" Then he closed his eyes.

The medical orderly and I frantically called to him, but he was gone. Tears streamed down our faces.

Slowly the Chairman extracted his arm from beneath Hu's neck, lowered him gently to the ground and stood up. In a low voice he said to me, "Coverlet."

I handed him the coverlet I had been carrying. He opened it and covered Comrade Hu carefully.

There wasn't a breath of wind that day. The trees and grass on the mountain were motionless. They seemed to be paying their last respects to the departed hero. We wiped away our tears and buried him. Then, following the Chairman, we marched on.

Snow Mountains and
Grasslands

IN June 1935, after crossing the Tatu River, we came
to the foot of Chiachin Mountain, a towering, snow-
covered peak. The June sun had not yet set but its heat
had lost its power in the face of this great icy mass.

We paused for a day at its foot. Chairman Mao had
advised us to collect ginger and chilli to fortify ourselves
against the bitter cold as we climbed the pass over the
mountain. We started the climb in the early morning of
the next day.

The peak of Chiachin Mountain pierced the sky like
a sword point glittering in the sunlight. Its whole mass
sparkled as if decorated with a myriad glittering mirrors.
Its brightness dazzled your eyes. Every now and again
clouds of snow swirled around the peak like a vast umbrella. It was an unearthly, fairyland sight.

At the start the snow was not so deep and we could walk on it fairly easily. But after twenty minutes or so the drifts became deeper and deeper. A single careless step could throw you into a crevasse and then it might take hours to extricate you. If you walked where the mantle of snow was lighter, it was slippery; for every step you took, you slid back three! Chairman Mao was walking ahead of us, his shoulders hunched, climbing with difficulty. Sometimes he would slip back several steps. Then we gave him a hand; but we too had difficulty in keeping our foothold and then it was he who caught our arms in a firm grip and pulled us up. He wore no padded clothes. Soon his thin grey trousers were wet through and his black cotton shoes were shiny with frost.

The climb was taking it out of us. I clambered up to him and said: "Chairman! It's too hard for you, better let us support you!" I stood firm beside him. But he only answered shortly: "No, you're just as tired as I am!" and went on.

Half way up the mountain a sudden, sharp wind blew up. Thick, dark clouds drifted along the top of the range. The gusts blew up the snow which swirled around us viciously.

I hurried a few steps forward and pulled at his jacket. "Snow's coming, Chairman!" I yelled.

He looked ahead against the wind. "Yes, it'll be on us almost at once. Let's get ready!" No sooner had he spoken than hailstones, as big as small eggs, whistled and splashed down on us. Umbrellas were useless against this gusty sea of snow and ice. We held an oilskin sheet up and huddled together under it with Chairman Mao in the centre. The storm raged around us as if the very sky were falling. All we could hear were the confused shouts of people, neighing of horses and deafening thunder claps. Then came a hoarse voice from above us.

"Comrades! Hold on! Don't give up! Persistence means victory!" I lifted my head and looked up. Red flags were flying from the top of the pass. I looked enquiringly at Chairman Mao.

"Who's that shouting there?"

"Comrades from the propaganda team," the Chairman replied. "We must learn from them. They've got a stubborn spirit!"

The snowstorm dropped as suddenly as it had started, and the warm, red sun came out again. Chairman Mao left the oilskin shelter and stood up on the snowy mountainside. The last snowflakes still whirled around him.

"Well, how did we come out of that battle?" he asked. "Anyone wounded?"

No one reported any hurts. Only Lao Yu led his horse up and announced, "A hailstone's made my arm swell up!"

Chairman Mao immediately called to Chung Fu-chang, the medical orderly, to put some salve on Lao Yu's arm. But Lao Yu smiled, refused any help and led his horse on. I was walking with Tseng Hsien-chi and teased him, "Well, chum, how do you like it?"

He pointed to Chairman Mao and said: "If he can take it, so can we!" Then he looked at his own feet buried deep in the snow and groaned jokingly: "Only

look at this stuff! It's confiscated my feet!" It was true
Numbed with the cold, it felt as if you had no feet!

As we went up higher, the going grew more difficult.
When we were still at the foot of the mountain, the local
people had told us: "When you get to the top of the
mountain, don't talk nor laugh, otherwise the god of the
mountain will choke you to death." We weren't super-
stitious, but there was some harsh truth in what they said.
Now I could hardly breathe. It seemed as if my chest
was being pressed between two millstones. My heartbeats
were fast and I had difficulty in talking, let alone laughing. I felt as if my heart would pop out of my mouth
if I opened it. Then I looked at Chairman Mao again.
He was walking ahead, stepping firmly against the wind
and snow. At the top of the mountain the propaganda
team shouted again:

"Comrades, step up! Look forward! Keep going!"

Finally we gained the summit of the mountain pass.
White snow blanketed everything. People sat in groups
of three or five. Some were so exhausted that they lay
down. When they saw Chairman Mao, several comrades
came up calling: "Chairman, come and take a rest!"

When Chairman Mao saw all this he immediately went
up to them and said gently: "Comrades, we can't rest
here! The air is too rarefied. Make another effort and
we'll meet the Fourth Front Army down on the other side."

With this, our spirits rose again, and we began to
scramble down the slope. I don't know whether it was
because of joy for the victory of reaching the top or for
some other reason, but suddenly I grew dizzy. It seemed

that the mountain shook beneath my feet. I lost control of my limbs and began to shiver violently. I stumbled up to Chairman Mao, cried out: "Chairman . . . !" and collapsed. But I was not wholly unconscious. I felt Chairman Mao supporting me with his arm and calling me by name. It was as if I was swimming in air. I had difficulty in breathing and could not speak. But a sudden strong wind lashed the snowflakes in my face. It brought me to and my eyes cleared. Comrades crowded around me wondering what was the matter. I heard Chairman Mao asking me: "What's wrong? Are you all right now?" I struggled to my feet and on we went.

Chairman Mao's feet plunged deep in the snow at every step. He turned his head to look at the comrades who still hadn't made it to the top. They walked slowly and the column looked like a snake winding its way to the summit. He waved them on encouragingly.

The wind was getting stronger and dark clouds were again gathering. As if urged on by an unknown power, I rushed to the Chairman and shouted, "Chairman, you can't stop here! Please go on quickly!"

Going down was easier than going up, but since there was no sunshine on this side of the mountain it was colder. We were all wearing the same thin cotton clothes, and we shivered with cold. I tied a blanket round my waist and so went walking, slipping and rolling down the snowy slopes.

Not long afterwards, we met comrades of the Fourth Front Army carrying banners with the words: "Expand the revolutionary base in northwestern Szechuan!" We

Finally we gained the summit of
the mountain pass. (p.69)

felt new strength come into our limbs. We felt for them as we would for brothers we had parted from long ago.

As we came down the last slopes, I turned back and looked upwards. The red flags were still fluttering on the top of the snow-covered mountain. The untiring voice of the propaganda comrades was still ringing in my ears.

*

*   *

Having made our way down Chiachin Mountain, we rested for a few days in Maokung. Then we climbed over another big snow mountain — Mengpi Mountain. We reached Chokechi in northwestern Szechuan, where we busied ourselves with preparations for crossing the grasslands. This done, we resumed our journey.

It was a cloudless morning when we left Chokechi. But before we were twenty *li* out, dark clouds came over and soon there was a fine drizzle coming down. We were passing a deserted mountain area full of strangely formed rocks. There was not even a small footpath to be seen among the sharp cliffs and pits of fallen leaves. A few moments later, a clap of thunder resounded and down came the rain. Big drops and falling twigs lashed us mercilessly. The Chairman's clothes and ours were soaked through.

By four o'clock in the afternoon it was dark. The downpour continued unabated. We were miles from any lodging place. The Chairman's riding lamp ran out of kerosene. We could not move a step in the pitch-dark. How urgently we needed light at this moment! As the Chairman made his way along with difficulty, looking very tired, I felt terribly uneasy. Just think! While others fell to sleep as soon as they reached a camping place, he would get busy attending meetings, reading telegrams, drafting documents, and so on. How energetic he was indeed!

"Let's stop here, Chairman," I proposed.

He stopped. After a moment's thought, he said, "Very well, tell everybody."

But now we were in trouble. All around us were water pits, rocks and darkness. Where could we fix up somewhere for him to sleep? But using our wits and putting forth some hard effort, we succeeded in improvising a "hammock" which we hung from two small trees.

Touching the wet hammock, the Chairman said humorously, "I'll be sleeping on a Kiangsi cooling bed!"

The Chairman's sense of humour cheered us up. Whenever we were beset with difficulties, a few light words from him invariably changed the atmosphere completely. His cheerful joking made us forget our weariness and injected us with new strength. We felt ready to face anything.

When the Chairman had lain down, we began to look for somewhere for ourselves. It was still raining. I felt around and touched a cliff. As my hand moved along it, I found a hole! A cave! I thought delightedly. Without further thought, I dived into it. Bang! My head hit something hard. It wasn't a cave, but merely a small hollow. But even this was something to be grateful for. Disregarding the pain, I lay down on my side with my head inside the opening. But why so much water on the ground? Feeling around with my hand, I found I was lying across a small pool of water. Oh, it didn't matter. I laid my small bundle across the mouth of the pool and used the Chairman's broken umbrella to keep the rain off my body. Though my head was exposed to the rain, I fell asleep as soon as it touched a rock.

When I woke up, the sun was out, shining through the dense foliage, although the morning mists were still lingering in the valleys. The rain had stopped and big drops were falling from the trees. No sooner had I opened my eyes than I felt a pain in my neck. It was a strange pain, which came only when I looked down. As the water dripped onto my face, all I could do was to let it run up my nostrils if I wanted to avoid the pain. I didn't take this too seriously as I thought it was nothing to fuss about. So I didn't say anything about it.

We continued our march.

Chairman Mao was always very observant. He was the first to see that something was wrong, and spoke to me in jest, "What's matter with you, Chen Chang-feng, looking up at the sky all the time? Are you looking out for planes?"

Gazing at the leaves above, I replied, "We've two skies over us here. Enemy planes can't find us no matter how clever they are."

"Then, what is it in the sky that holds so much interest for you?" was his next question.

I walked up to him. "There's something wrong with my neck," said I. "I can't look down. Each time I try to move my head I get a terrible pain."

The Chairman stopped at once. "It's nothing serious," I went on. "It'll be all right after a while." I didn't want to worry him.

Ignoring my last remarks, he touched my neck gently and turned to call Chung Fu-chang, the medical orderly, to come at once and attend to me.

Now everybody was aroused. I was surrounded. Tseng Hsien-chi and the porter Chung Yung-ho took a particular interest in my ailment. They pressed my neck and felt my head, bothering me so much that I was agitated beyond words.

Chung Fu-chang examined me very carefully. Then he turned to the Chairman with a smile. "I can't do anything for this patient," he said, "he must've cricked his neck in the night!"

The Chairman looked somewhat relieved. "Still, we have to do something for him. Tseng Hsien-chi, go to the medical corps and ask the doctor to come and see Chen Chang-feng."

Before I could say "not necessary," Tseng Hsien-chi was off.

To prevent me from falling while walking along with my face turned upwards, the Chairman took me by the hand like a father leading a child just learning to walk.

"Don't worry," he said, trying to comfort me. "You'll be all right!"

The doctor came hurrying up, asked me a lot of detailed questions, tried my neck and rubbed in some ointment. In a short time the neck was feeling easier.

"Are you all right now?" asked the Chairman, when he saw I could bend my head again.

I nodded and told him that I was all right, whereupon he said, "You're a wonder! For the sake of sleep, you're willing to give up your head!"

*

* *

Leaving the forests and mountains behind us, we arrived in Maoerhkai. Here we made a stop to complete preparations for crossing the grasslands on the Chinghai-Sikang border.

I began to suffer badly from malaria. I had contracted it, before we crossed Chiachin Mountain, but had no attacks while crossing the mountain. Then I got a drenching and now, exhausted by the long march, I was down with a sharp attack just as we made ready to overcome one of the most difficult obstacles in our path — the grasslands with their treacherous quagmires. To be sick at such a time was not only a personal misfortune; I would be a burden and a worry to all my comrades and especially Chairman Mao. He too was weaker now and his slim figure appeared to be taller than ever.

He was attending many meetings at this time. Sometimes they lasted till late at night and then without any rest he went on discussing problems with leading comrades until far into the small hours. Busy though he was, he often came to see me. When he saw I was in low spirits he would encourage me by explaining why we had to cross these grasslands and enliven me by recounting interesting stories that he knew.

I felt in him the love of a father. I felt a warm and deep gratitude to him and I bitterly reproached myself. How could I go and get sick at such a time? I had added to my comrades' burdens and distracted the attention of our Chairman.

We spent about a month at Maoerhkai. Then finally in mid-August of 1935, we started out for the great grasslands that had never before been crossed by human beings. We hadn't gone forty *li* before we came to a huge primeval forest. Its trees, with immensely thick trunks, towered above us. When we stopped for the night we would sling Chairman Mao's hammock between two trees, but he would rarely rest in it. He would be off at meetings or visiting the men. So Chung Fu-chang, the medical orderly, let me rest in it.

I was lying there one night when it was already dark. The troops had lit many bonfires. Neither birds nor animals had probably ever seen fire before in this ancient forest. They were scared, made strange noises and flew or prowled around in panic. My comrades were sleeping around a nearby fire.

I had Chairman Mao's blanket over me and wore a new suit that he had given to me at Maoerhkai, but suddenly I felt a bout of uncontrollable shivering coming on. As I shivered violently, I told myself not to groan so as not to wake the others. I was specially afraid of disturbing Chung Fu-chang, the medical orderly, because if he knew I had a malarial attack he would immediately tell Chairman Mao who would then refuse to use his own hammock. I held my breath, doubled my knees up to my chin and kept silent. Suddenly I noticed a tall shadow in front of me. Chairman Mao had come back! I struggled to stretch out my legs but they were numbed and refused to move. I couldn't control my limbs. My teeth chattered. I was shivering like a man in a fit. The Chairman came up to the hammock and bent over me.

"What's wrong, Chen Chang-feng?" He put his hand on me and cried out, "Chung Fu-chang! Chen Chang-feng is sick again!" He didn't speak very loud, but everyone around the fire woke up and they all crowded round me.

When I saw Chairman Mao and the other comrades around me looking at me with such concern, strength seemed to return to my body and I was able to sit up.

"You lie down," ordered the Chairman gently and used his two hands to press me back into the hammock. I struggled to sit upright, but that pair of powerful hands forced me back. I lost my strength to resist. When he saw that I was quiet again he told Chung Fu-chang to give me some medicine. Then he and the other comrades went back to the fireside to sleep.

The next morning as soon as I woke up, I jumped off the hammock. I didn't know where my strength came from — perhaps from the night's good sleep or perhaps from the inspiration of the Chairman's fatherly care. The first thing I did was to run to see him.

"Are you feeling better?" he asked, putting his hands on my arms.

I couldn't speak a word. I was in tears.

We continued our march. The ancient forest was left behind and we entered the grasslands. A vast stretch of desolate marsh confronted us. Not a single human being lived here. There were no houses. Wild grasses grew in profusion in the stagnant water. There seemed to be no end to it. The sodden earth squelched monotonously *pu-chi, pu-chi,* as we laboured over it. A careless step could send you to a fearful death in its muddy depths, trap your feet in a morass. Once caught it was difficult to pull your legs out of the quagmire without the help of your comrades. More than once the Chairman helped some of us with his strong hands.

The weather was cold and changeable. Now it rained, now it snowed. Sometimes it hailed. Every step was an effort. Chairman Mao was walking ahead of us. He would stop for a moment now and again, look back with great concern and call our names until we all answered him. Then he would go on. Sometimes when he saw we were tired he would tell us stories and jokes and make us burst out laughing. And we forgot our tiredness.

No one grumbled or complained. We were determined to pull through and we were confident we could do it. Indeed, we were always optimistic in the company of Chairman Mao.

The troops too had entered the grasslands. They wore a motley set of uniforms. Some were in field grey, others wore greatcoats made of various pelts, some had flung blankets over themselves as capes. Some wore large round hats of plaited bamboo, others carried battered umbrellas. But this tatterdemalion throng brought life to these dead marshes. They marched linked together hand in hand in long lines, advancing slowly but steadily.

One day we suddenly noticed a black spot on the otherwise desolate horizon. It grew larger and larger as we advanced. And our excitement grew with it. Hope welled in our hearts. It was Panyu. I can't describe our feelings. When we finally reached it, Chairman Mao and we bodyguards took up billets in a house belonging to a Tibetan family. Our men were elated. We lit fires of cowdung to dry our wet and mildewed clothes.

Soon afterwards we arrived in Pahsi, and here we witnessed a strange scene: some men of the Fourth Front Army were marching slowly and dejectedly in the opposite direction to us, towards the grasslands! We couldn't understand this and asked Chairman Mao the reason. He didn't reply immediately, but from the expression on his face we could see that he was deeply stirred. Then he told us. This was the result of the intrigue of the renegade Chang Kuo-tao to split the Party. It was he, like a slave driver, who was forcing these innocent comrades to take this road of destruction.

After a while Chairman Mao asked us: "Do you want to turn back and recross the grasslands?"

"Never, we'd rather face death," we replied with one voice.

The Chairman stood up and looked back at those shabby, tired figures marching back to where we had come from. He spoke in a low but confident voice: "They'll come back! We must open a way ahead for them so that they can come to us!"

On Mount Liupan

A T dusk in the middle of September, we arrived at a village close to Latsekou. I spread the Chairman's pallet so that he could get some rest. But when I went into the next room, he was already in conference with Nieh Jung-chen, Liu Ya-lou and other leaders. The table was spread with maps.

Latsekou, known as a strategic pass, connects the provinces of Szechuan and Kansu, and was one of the major passes we had to get through to reach northern Shensi. I was sure this was what the Chairman and the others were discussing, so I withdrew without a word. The Chairman didn't get to sleep until very late that night.

But we attacked the pass the next morning at dawn. After taking it we didn't linger, but pushed on.

At the end of September, we crossed the Weishui River blockade line and headed for Mount Liupan.

Mount Liupan, a spur of the Lungshan Range, is the highest peak in western Kansu. It was also the last big mountain we had to cross to get to northern Shensi. When the men heard they were to cross the mountain, their spirits rose.

The sky was cloudy and a cold wind blew the day we set out to climb it. Soon it started to rain. But although we were soaked by the time we reached the foothills nothing could dampen our determination.

Mount Liupan couldn't be compared with snow-covered Chiachin Mountain, which we had already cross-ed. But when we stood at its base and peered up, it looked dangerous enough. The trail twisted and turned. At the start of the climb there were small trees we could grab. But as we neared the summit, there was nothing, only clumps of withered grass. It was very tough going.

I was still weak from the malaria. The trail was about thirty *li* to the top and very uneven. By the time we were halfway up, I was gasping for breath. My heart was pumping hard and I was drenched with sweat.

Chairman Mao quickly noticed the shape I was in. Whenever we came to a difficult stretch, he extended his big strong hand and pulled me along.

As we neared the top, I couldn't go another step. My head swam, my body seemed to float and I suddenly collapsed in a heap.

I was vaguely aware of two large hands helping me to my feet, and I heard Chairman Mao's kindly voice say to Tseng, "Get the medical orderly to give him some medicine in a hurry. His malaria has come back."

Soon someone put two bitter tablets into my mouth, and I was given a drink of water. I gradually recovered.

Chairman Mao was supporting me, and Tseng and the medical orderly were watching. My heart sank. "It's not malaria, Chairman," I cried. "It's just that I have no strength. I'm afraid I'll never get to northern Shensi."

"You will, definitely. Don't worry," the Chairman said encouragingly. "There's nothing frightening about difficulties. The only thing to worry about is being afraid of them. They're pretty frightening if you are. But they're not the least bit if you don't let them scare you. Stick it out. Once we get over this mountain you'll be all right."

The Chairman's words gave me confidence. But I didn't want to be a burden to him. "You go on ahead, Chairman," I said. "I'll follow as soon as I've had a little rest."

"Nothing doing," the Chairman said firmly. "The air is very thin up here, and it's raining. You can't rest here. You've got to hold out until we get over this mountain, no matter what."

He and Tseng carried me and continued on. The Chairman was so concerned, I wanted to walk, but I was shivering all over. I couldn't move a step.

"Are you cold?" the Chairman asked.

"Chilled to the bone."

"Here, put this coat on and drink some more hot water. You'll feel better when you warm up a bit." The Chairman took off his overcoat.

All he had on underneath was a grey cotton army uniform which had been made for him when we were in Tsunyi. What's more, he had worked until very late the night before and had marched for hours today in the rain. Not only hadn't I taken good care of the Chairman, in fact I had added to his burdens. How could I accept his coat?

I pushed it back. "I don't need it. I can march." I refused to put it on, and struggled to walk. But I was too weak. I took one step and collapsed in a faint.

When I opened my eyes again, I was wearing the Chairman's coat. The Chairman stood in the rain, the autumn wind ruffling his thin grey army tunic. He was still looking rather worried about me, but a smile had begun to brighten his expression.

Tseng brought me a bowl of drinking water and stood by my side.

Warmth flooded through me. My strength seemed to return. I rose to my feet and stared at the Chairman. My throat was constricted.

The Chairman was delighted. "Feeling better?"

"Fine. Let's go." There was so much I wanted to say, but this was all I could manage.

"Good. You're a real Red Army soldier." Chairman Mao fondly patted me on the shoulder. "Let's go."

By dusk we finally crossed Mount Liupan and reached the foot of the other side. I looked back up.

"You see, you made it," said the Chairman. "That's the way to deal with difficulties."

We camped in a village at the foot of the mountain that night. I lay on my bed, thinking of all that had happened that day. "If it weren't for the Chairman's care and encouragement, I probably would have died on Mount Liupan today," I said to myself.

I thought and thought, and tears filled my eyes. "I'll never forget what the Chairman said," I vowed. "No matter where or when, I'll remember, always."

We Are Home!

AFTER crossing Mount Liupan, we entered the Hui region of Kansu. The Hui people were very warm to us. Wherever we went they streamed out to welcome us along the roadside, handing us bowls of hot water and saying, "Where did you come from? You must be tired, comrades. Please drink some hot water." We had seldom heard people talk to us in the Han language since we entered the Tibetan region, so we felt especially at home here in the Hui region when we were addressed as "comrades". We gathered from them that our Red 25th Army, which had passed through here in July, had left them a very good impression with its rigorous discipline. As we were getting nearer to northern Shensi, our excitement made us forget all our fatigue and ailments. We wished we could step onto the soil of Shensi at once to see our future "home".

One day soon after we started out from Huanhsien County in Kansu, we found ourselves on a small path skirting a mountain. Suddenly we saw five men on horse-back galloping towards us. Clearly friends, they carried Mausers on their hips and wore white towels on their heads. When they came up, we saw they were sturdy, young chaps in their twenties. When they reached the foot of the mountain, they alighted and walked towards us. "Where's Chairman Mao?" they asked us loudly.

I went to meet them and asked them what they wanted.

An older man among them, breathing heavily and with sweat all over his face, said in a warm voice: "We're sent by Old Liu to deliver a letter to Chairman Mao. Where is he?"

Old Liu! Wasn't that Comrade Liu Chih-tan?

"Comrades," I asked, "are you sent by Comrade Liu Chih-tan?"

"Exactly," they said in one voice. Meanwhile the older man handed me the letter. I hurried with it to the Chairman. When the Chairman read it he smiled and said, "Comrades, you've done good work!" Then they knew it was he — Chairman Mao — whom the people of northern Shensi had expected to see for a long time. They crowded round, struggling to shake hands with him.

The Chairman walked up to where the troops were resting. Standing in their midst, he spoke loudly, "Comrades, we are about to reach the Soviet area in northern Shensi! Our 25th and 26th Armies have defeated the enemy's second encirclement campaign and sent men to meet us!"

Tumultuous cheers broke out at this announcement. Everyone was shouting, laughing and flinging his arms around another.

The five comrades who had come to meet us acted as our guides, leading us into a village called Sanchachen. That evening the Chairman talked with them for a long while and wrote a letter for them. He did not even have time to eat.

The following day we stopped at a small village whose name we did not know. There was no rice to be bought, only golden-coloured millet. We bodyguards being all southerners had never seen millet before, let alone cook it. What to do? Since there were plenty of goats, we bought a big one and prepared a mutton dinner.

"Why only meat?" the Chairman wanted to know, when the leg of mutton we had reserved for him was brought in.

"We couldn't get any rice in this village nor any flour," said Tseng Hsien-chi quickly. "There's only millet but we don't know how to cook it."

"Learn to do it; it isn't difficult," said the Chairman. "We've to learn new ways of living when we come to a new place. Otherwise, we'll starve to death."

We made as though to go and cook the millet on the spot. "There's no hurry for it," said the Chairman. "Let's have the mutton on its own this time!"

During the 80-*li* journey between Chuchih and the dividing ridge on the Kansu-Shensi border, we fought some 18 battles with the cavalry under Kuomintang warlord Ma Hung-kuei. But as soon as we contacted Ma's horsemen, they would gallop away. We used to laugh at them saying that they couldn't even measure up to the "bean-curd" troops (meaning, as soft as bean-curd) under Kweichow warlord Wang Chia-lieh; they were only the refuse from the beans after making the curd!

The Chairman's wry comments on these troops tickled our sense of humour. "They wouldn't dare to fight when they know it's the Chinese Workers' and Peasants' Red Army," he remarked. "They are only 'expert' in running away!"

On the top of the ridge stood a large tablet with bold characters "Dividing Ridge", marking the border between Kansu and Shensi Provinces. We sat down for a rest under a chestnut tree near the tablet.

The Chairman was reading the characters on the back of the tablet. "We have crossed ten provinces already," he told us elatedly. "When we go down this mountain, we'll be in the eleventh province — Shensi. That's our base area — our home!"

A day and a half's march from the dividing ridge brought us to Wuchi Town where we stayed in the cave rooms cut in the side of the loess hills. It was the first time in our lives we had seen such caves. We were now in the Soviet area.

The Chairman got busy conferring with leading comrades on how to dispose of Ma Hung-kuei's cavalry.

Our soldiers were excited at the thought of the coming battle. "We're getting near home," they said. "Let's present the people of northern Shensi with a gift in the form of a victory!"

The big day came. We stood with the Chairman on a mountain top which was bare of all vegetation. As the battle began, our machine-guns rattled. The frightened horses bolted in all directions neighing and attempting to escape the hail of bullets, throwing their riders and rolling down the slopes with them. Those who survived ran for their lives.

It was a real treat to watch the battle from the "grand stand". "Chairman!" we exclaimed. "We've only got two legs and they've got four, but we've made them run all over the mountain!" He joined in our general burst of laughter.

While the troops were taking a rest in Wuchi Town, we accompanied the Chairman to Hsiashihwan, the seat of the Shensi-Kansu Provincial Party Committee and the Provincial Soviet.

Large snowflakes were falling when we set out. Although we weren't wearing too many clothes, nobody felt the cold as we trudged over the rough mountain paths. It was dusk when we reached Hsiashihwan. We heard the beating of gongs and drums and the noise of a crowd of people. From a distance we could see a large gathering on a spacious ground at the entrance to the village. The people were waiting to welcome the Chairman. As soon as they caught sight of him, they cheered madly. Amidst a tremendous din of gongs and drums, the crowd rushed up, waving small red and green banners bearing the words:

Welcome Chairman Mao!
Welcome the Central Red Army!

Expand the Shensi-Kansu-Ningsia Soviet Area!
Smash the enemy's third encirclement campaign!
Long live the Chinese Communist Party!

In his worn overcoat which he had brought along from Kiangsi, and his old cap, the Chairman nodded and waved at the crowd again and again. Then the people cleared a way for a score of leading comrades to come up and shake hands with the Chairman. They included Comrades Liu Chih-tan and Hsu Hai-tung, Commander of the 25th Red Army. Standing with Chairman Mao to receive the welcomers were Comrades Chou En-lai, Tung Pi-wu, Hsu Teh-li, Lin Po-chu and Hsieh Chueh-tsai. They shook hands all around and introduced one another.

"Welcome to Chairman Mao!" the crowd cheered. Shouts rose from every corner, shaking the very earth.

"We've won through! We've won through!" Tseng Hsien-chi and I also shouted.

Chairman Mao
Sends Me to School

WE soon settled down after arriving in northern Shensi.

In the spring of 1936, Comrade Mo Wen-hua, Director of the Political Department of the Red Army Academy, came to see Chairman Mao and talked about recruiting students for the academy. During their talk, the Chairman looked across at me meditatively and said: "There are some veterans here at headquarters. They are good comrades who passed the test of the Long March. How about sending some of them to you to study?" Comrade Mo nodded his consent and said: "They're welcome, warmly welcome!"

One morning, a few days later, I was going out after bringing the Chairman's washing water, when he stopped me and said: "Chen Chang-feng! I'm sending you to the Red Army Academy to study! How's that?"

I didn't answer immediately. My heart beat fast. All sorts of thoughts crowded into my mind. I who had never been to school, who had herded cattle for the landlords in my childhood, was to be sent to a real school! Of course I was glad! But I had been with him about six years. This was not a short time. During the most difficult days, no matter how busy he was, he always had a thought for me and taught me. He had concerned himself with my political and general education and everyday troubles, down to the trifles of life. It was under his fatherly care that I gradually learned the truth about class struggle and many other things. But what was most important was that from his own daily life and work I had learned what a real Communist was. . . .

Seeing my hesitation, the Chairman asked me again, "Have you made up your mind?"

"I . . . I don't think I should go, Chairman."

"Why?"

"Nothing except that I don't want to leave you. Besides, won't it be just as good to learn from you?"

The Chairman came close to me, put his hand on my shoulder and told me to sit down. Seating himself beside me, he began in a soft tone, "Chen Chang-feng, you should understand that our revolutionary base is expanding day by day. We need cadres to do all kinds of work — cadres loyal to the Party, loyal to the people. You've been with me about six years now. You haven't had much opportunity to study. Now you should go to a school where you can study systematically. When you've finished your studies, you'll be able to work better for the Party, and I'll be very happy. What do you say?"

He kept looking at me with great affection as he spoke.

"But, if I'm gone, who'll look after you?" I knew it was a childish question even as I asked it.

"You don't have to worry about that," he said, smiling. "When you're gone, someone else will be sent here to take your place."

I stood up, so flustered that I carried away the water basin before the Chairman had a chance to wash in it. I discovered my absent-mindedness only when my tears dropped into the clean unused water.

So the question of my going to school was settled. I spent a sleepless night before I left the Chairman, thinking of the importance of study, my coming school life and the Chairman. "Who will take my place? Since the new comrade will not get to know the Chairman's habits very soon, will he take good care of our beloved leader?" The very thought set my mind in a turmoil again. I jumped out of bed and walked out. It was very late; the light was still burning in the Chairman's room. I decided to make a last request to let me stay with him. But when I approached the window and saw him writing, my courage evaporated. I knew if I went in, he would talk with me. Years of experience told me that I should not interrupt his work. What was my small problem compared with his work which had to do with the whole country, whole Party? I tiptoed back to my living quarters.

I got up very early the next morning. As usual I went to the Chairman's office to clean and sweep and put things to rights — the job I knew so well. But now I was parting with all these things.

The Chairman came in holding some paper pads and pencils. "You'll soon be going," he said. "Never mind the room. Take a rest." Handing me the pads and pencils, he continued, "These are for you to use in the school. Study well. Come and see me when you've time."

I took over the Chairman's gifts. Gazing at him, I felt my throat tightening up and my eyes filling. I couldn't utter a single word.

*

*   *

Chairman Mao went to the front soon after I entered the Red Army Academy. I studied there altogether forty days and was then transferred to the Northwest Security Bureau as instructor to a security detachment. In August that same year Chairman Mao returned from the Shansi front and I went to visit him. The moment I entered the room his first question to me was about my studies.

"I'm not studying any longer; I'm working now," I replied.

"What kind of work?" the Chairman asked me, lighting a cigarette and settling down for a talk. I told him.

"Fine! How many men have you got?"

"Over two hundred."

When the Chairman heard this he looked up at me quizzically and teased me. "Over two hundred! That means that you're a small battalion commander!" (At that time many of our companies had only seventy to eighty men each.)

I felt embarrassed at the Chairman's remark.

"Are you getting on well at your job?" was his next question. "As an instructor have you learned how to stand at attention and at ease?"

Remembering that as young fellows in the service of the Chairman we had made a poor showing when we stood at attention or at ease — that was what the Chairman now had in mind — I replied with a smile: "Yes, I've learned. But I still can't make a speech, especially at roll-call in the evening. . . ."

He smiled and asked: "When you're talking, do the men stamp their feet and complain about the mosquitoes?"

At that time if the usual speech during the evening roll-call was too long and dull, some jokers in the ranks would be sure to stamp their feet and if you asked them what was the matter, they'd say that the mosquitoes were biting them. Chairman Mao, it seemed, was well aware of our army jokes.

He then said seriously: "Now that you're a cadre you must be alert. When you're talking, make things clear; don't gabble. Don't put on airs; don't act!" Then he asked: "Are your men learning to read and write?"

I answered "Yes," and when he asked me who taught them I answered "I." "So you're the teacher!" he exclaimed. "How can you teach others when you know so few characters yourself?"

"I'm teaching while learning," I explained. "When there's any word I don't know I look it up in the Students' Pocket Dictionary."

When the Chairman heard this, he encouraged me: "That's good! Work hard and overcome difficulties! You remember when we were in Kiangsi how Hsieh Chueh-tsai, Hsu Teh-li and Tso Chuan taught you to read and write?"

I nodded. How could I forget? In those Kiangsi days, as soon as we settled down in some place the leading cadres would take turns to give us lectures and teach us how to read and write. Comrade Hsieh Chueh-tsai, for one, took a special interest in our studies. Chairman Mao, busy though he was, would do all he could to help our studies whenever he had a moment to spare.

At that time, as later, wherever the Red Army went, it would post up slogans. Chairman Mao would help us to learn the characters in these slogans and later examine us. It was he who held my hand and taught me to write my own name. He taught us all sorts of other things as well. When we were in Lungyen in Fukien, a coal-mining centre, he told us how coal was formed underground. When we came to some hot-springs, he explained the reason for them. When there was thunder and lightning he told us what these were.

When we were in Juichin, Kiangsi, the Chairman had the same monthly allowance for vegetables as all of us. He had no cook. Wu Chieh-ching and I took turns to buy and cook his food. When I returned from the market,

I would put the names of the vegetables in my notebook. One day he saw these lists and asked me:

"Are these your accounts?"

"No," I replied, "these are words I am learning."

"That's a good way to learn characters," he commented. "Does Wu Chieh-ching do this, too?"

When I answered "No," he said, "That's too bad. Tell him to come here!"

I called in Wu and the Chairman told him, "From now on when you buy vegetables, be sure to write down the accounts and report to me!"

That got Wu reading and writing seriously.

This was kind of deep interest Chairman Mao took in our education.

I Bid Chairman Mao Goodbye

AFTER the War of Resistance Against Japan was concluded in our victory, the Party sent a large number of cadres to the newly recovered areas where the people were awaiting us to carry out new tasks. At that time I was the Chief of the Tungkuan Sub-Office of the Bureau of Public Security in Yenan. One day I was called by the Party's Central Organization Department for a discussion about my new job. When I went there, I was told by a comrade of that department that the Party was considering to send me to the front and I was asked to choose between Shantung and the Northeast.

One of the important things demanded of a member of the Communist Party is to carry out the Party's orders. I would go to any place the Party needed me. So I left the Party to decide for me.

The Party decided that I should go to Shantung to work.

In the past when I was transferred to a new job, I had never felt so uneasy as I was now. This time I was leaving Yenan for a place far away and probably I would not be able to see the Chairman for a long while. When I came back home, my first thought was to see him to say good-bye. I phoned him and he gave me an appointment the next morning.

Throughout that night I was wide awake with excitement. I chatted with my wife. I told her about my childhood, my days with the Chairman, his care for me, his plain style of living, his loyalty to the Party and the people. . . .

The following day immediately after breakfast I set off accompanied by my wife and year-old baby. When we arrived in Wangchiaping, where he lived, Ho Ching-hua, his bodyguard, told us: "Chairman Mao has been waiting for you since early morning in his office!"

We followed him into the courtyard. Comrade Chiang Ching, Chairman Mao's wife, came out to welcome us. She shook hands with us and took the baby in her arms. The Chairman was soon with us. In a loose-fitting uniform, he looked a bit stouter now. I saluted him as in the old days. He invited us into his room and when we were seated, asked me: "Where are you going?"

I told him I was going to Shantung.

"So you're leaving northern Shensi! Do you have any difficulties?"

I answered, "No." Then he asked me if my wife and baby were accompanying me and if we expected any difficulties on the way. When I had answered his questions, Chairman Mao admonished me to take good care of them.

Then he talked with my wife. He was pleased to know that we had a happy home life.

He played with the baby and asked us all about her. He talked about my transfer to Shantung, saying that when one went to work in a new place, one was bound to meet with difficulties. "It's up to you to find ways to overcome them," he said and told me again, "Keep close contact with the masses!" As he talked he called Ho Ching-hua who brought in two packets of biscuits and some preserved beef. Handing them to me he said: "Now you are leaving. I've nothing nice to give you but here is something for the child on the journey." On my part, I took out a small notebook and asked him: "Chairman Mao, I'm leaving you; will you write something in my notebook for me?"

He immediately wrote the following lines in my notebook:

To Comrade Chang-feng,

Work hard. Be loyal to the Party and to the people! I wish you every success.

Mao Tsetung

May 17, 1946

He also gave me a photograph of himself.

As I understood from Ho Ching-hua that the Chairman was about to go to a meeting, my wife and I got ready to leave.

"No hurry," said the Chairman. "Stay here for lunch while I go to the meeting." He told Ho to prepare the lunch and let me select some dishes.

We said that as we had to prepare for the journey, we couldn't stay for lunch.

The Chairman walked out with us, telling me again and again to work well and take good care of myself. As he stretched out his hand I gripped it hard. I could not say a word.

I left Yenan on May 18, 1946. Over the many years that have passed since then, whether fighting in the front lines or working for peaceful construction, I always feel I'm still with the Chairman. My strength and confidence increase whenever I think of him. His photograph and my notebook with his parting message in it I still keep with me to this day. I will always do as he said — put my best efforts into my work and remain loyal to the Party and the people.

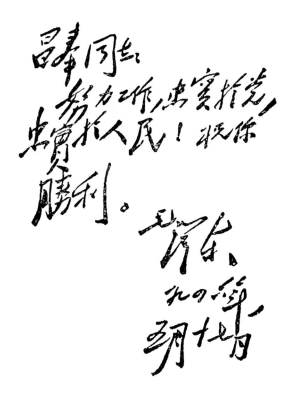

Chairman Mao's autograph in the author's notebook

To Comrade Chang-feng,

Work hard. Be loyal to the Party and to the people! I wish you every success.

Mao Tsetung

May 17, 1946

Happy Reminiscences

TWELVE years have passed since I left Chairman Mao at Yenan. It was on May 17, 1946, I remember, that I went to say goodbye to him before I left for Shantung. He had a good talk with me.

"So you're going to Shantung?" the Chairman began. "That's a good place. We have a large revolutionary base there. As we've lately liberated many counties, cadres are needed to do different kinds of work. When you go there, be sure to respect the local responsible leaders and those in the organization to which you've been transferred. You must unite and co-operate well with the cadres in the locality."

Having listened attentively to his advice, I took out my notebook and asked him to write a few words. He did (as seen in the plate) and autographed the photo he gave me. I have treasured them ever since.

I remember the days when I began to serve the Chairman, first as orderly and then as bodyguard and how I

went with him through the Long March. I was then
sixteen. As a matter of fact, the Chairman was taking
care of me instead of me taking care of him. He explained
to me the truths of revolution, taught me how to read
and write and wrote letters home for me whenever I
thought of my folks. On night marches under heavy
rain, he would take over the storm lantern and lead the
way with it so that I would not fall. An unforgettable
incident was when I fell sick with malaria for several
days while passing Mount Liupan. I was then very weak.
Before I reached the mountain top, I began to shake all
over and then fainted. The Chairman took off his worn
overcoat for me to wear while he stood in the cold wind
in his thin clothes.

But my political education was a matter of even greater
concern to him than my physical comfort. When I was
leaving him to go to the Red Army Academy in February
1936, he said to me earnestly, "It's a good thing to study,
not because you want to get an official position but because you'll be able to do more work for the people. Of
course, you'll have some difficulties in your studies, too.
But as long as you've made up your mind to serve the
people, you'll overcome all difficulties."

I was still like a boy when I worked in the Yenan
Bureau of Public Security. Whenever I had a chance,
I would go to the Chairman to have a heart-to-heart talk.
At that time I attached a good deal of importance to rank
and position. I felt that I deserved promotion after
working as an instructor for over four years. Once I said

to the Chairman, "Chairman, how much longer do you think I should remain an instructor?"

"Being an instructor is also a revolutionary work. Do you think you should be an official?" he asked me. "The Communist Party is not the place for anybody who is only out to be an official. We're all the same, we work for the people — whether as an official or not. No one will get anywhere here if he's after promotion, or out to make a fortune."

I found these words very inspiring. They made a deep impression on me. Through all the years since I left Yenan for Shantung, whenever I've been transferred from one post to another, I've worked in high spirits in any position without personal consideration because I've taken the Chairman's words as my motto and source of strength.

It's twelve years now since I bid Chairman Mao goodbye, and I have often longed to see him. During the war years when the liberated areas were cut off by the enemy communications were difficult, so I could only write to him. Since the nation-wide victory, I would very much have liked to go to Peking and pay him a visit. But on account of work, I've been unable to do so.

One day in February 1953 while I was attending a military training class in Nanking, I received an order to assemble with my classmates and go to send off a certain leading comrade. This leading comrade, I discovered, was none other than Chairman Mao. I was terribly excited. As he passed us in review and walked up to the gunboat, waving goodbye to the crowd on the shore, I itched to break ranks and run up to have a word with him. Of course, it couldn't be done. All I could do was watch the boat draw out from the wharf and slowly disappear from sight.

Some time later when the regulations providing leave for army officers came into effect, I began to save up in preparation for making the best use of my leave and fulfilling my long-felt wish by visiting the Chairman in Peking.

But I was in for a pleasant surprise. August 9, 1958 was the great day. While I was attending an army Party congress in Tsinan, Shantung Province, Chairman Mao came to meet the delegates. When I saw him stepping out of the motor-car I was overjoyed, as I was sure I'd be able to talk with him this time. I fidgeted restlessly while he was sitting with us to have a photograph taken, thinking of what to say to him. Then somebody must have told him that I was in the group. He asked for me. In great haste I went up to him. As I saluted, I forgot all that I meant to say. I was tongue-tied with emotion. It was he who spoke first, "It's Chen Chang-feng, isn't it?"

"Yes," I muttered.

He held out his hand which I clasped in both of mine. I was so excited that I even forgot to ask him how he was.

"It's over ten years since we parted," the Chairman began. "How are you?"

"It's twelve years!" I managed to say. "Are you well, Chairman?"

"Where are you working?"

"In a sub-military zone," I replied.

Political Director Li and Deputy Director Tung who were standing beside me told the Chairman that I was a deputy commander of a sub-military zone.

"So you're a commander now!" the Chairman said with a smile. "Have you been home?"

"I was back once in 1953."

"Was it your old home in Ningtu?"

He certainly had a wonderful memory! After so many years he still remembered that my home was in Ningtu. I told him it was.

"How's your family and who are your family members now?"

I told him all about my family — how they had joined the agricultural co-operative and how their living conditions had improved, and so on.

"How many children have you now?"

"Four."

"Fine!" Apparently he was glad to know it. Next he asked, "How old are you now?"

"Over forty," said I.

"Forty what?"

"Forty-four!"

He burst out laughing. "Not so young!"

Clasping my hand in both of his, he said, "Very good! We'll see each other again!"

His grip was strong. He was certainly in far better health than before. He wore a white shirt, grey trousers and old leather shoes, and was as simple and easy to approach as ever. I watched his imposing figure walking firmly towards the car which was waiting to take him away.

The day's pleasant surprise gave me a sleepless night. I lay awake turning over memories in my mind which took me back to the Chairman's side as in the old days.

About the Long March

THE Chinese Workers' and Peasants' Red Army took two whole years (October 1934 - October 1936) to complete its world-renowned Long March from the southern bases of Fukien and Kiangsi to northern Shensi, covering a distance of 25,000 *li*, or 12,500 kilometres. Fighting its way through eleven provinces, the Red Army scaled snow-covered mountains and strategic passes, forced treacherous rivers and traversed untrodden grasslands, while breaking through the enemy's cordons of hundreds of thousands strong. The fighters' unrivalled bravery and stamina spoke volumes for the fighting strength of the people's army under the leadership of the Communist Party, which proves invincible before all enemies.

Following is an account of how the Long March had come about and ended in victory, and its historic significance.

*
*   *

When in 1931 the Japanese imperialists occupied the Northeast, China was faced with a critical situation. The Kuomintang regime, however, ignoring the demand of the people to resist the Japanese invaders and save the country, adopted a policy of non-resistance towards the Japanese. They concentrated their attacks on the revolutionary bases led by the Chinese Communist Party.

In October 1933, Chiang Kai-shek gathered together a million troops and launched his fifth campaign of encirclement against the revolutionary bases — mainly the central base in Kiangsi Province with Juichin as the centre. By then, the Red Army throughout the country had grown to 300,000 men; and the civilian armed forces had also greatly developed. Food and other materials were in better supply than before. The thoroughgoing agrarian reform in the revolutionary bases, the progress of economic construction and the improvement in the living conditions of the people made the masses — especially the peasants — even more enthusiastic in backing the revolutionary war.

In November of that year, the "Fukien Incident" occurred. The 19th Route Army, originally under Kuomintang command, led by Tsai Ting-kai, joined with Li Chi-shen and other Kuomintang members to form the "People's Revolutionary Government of the Chinese Republic" in Fukien, and signed an agreement with the Red Army to oppose Chiang Kai-shek and resist the Japanese aggressors. As a result, the Red Army had more advantageous conditions in this campaign against encirclement than in the previous four.

Unfortunately, the Communist Party was then under the domination of the third "Left" line. The "Left" opportunists who were in control of the Party, after entering the central revolutionary base at the beginning of 1933, overrode Comrade Mao Tsetung and took over the leadership of the bases and of the Red Army. They did not co-operate well with the 19th Route Army, so that the latter, left to fend for itself, was annihilated by Chiang Kai-shek. But, what was more serious, they negated the correct strategy of Comrade Mao Tsetung and practised adventurism in the offensive by advocating regular and positional warfare in the face of the better-equipped Kuomintang armies, thus bringing enormous losses to the Red Army. Later they switched to conservatism in the defensive by carrying out the so-called all-out defensive and scattering the forces, which landed the Red Army in a passive position. Although after a year's bitter struggle the Red Army had won some partial military successes, it could not break the enemy encirclement. On the contrary, the bases were contracting and the Red Army was becoming more and more exhausted.

Under such conditions, in order to preserve its strength and fight against Japanese aggression in the north, the Red Army decided there was no alternative but to break through the enemy cordon and undertake the Long March.

In October 1934, the main force of the First Front Army, totalling 85,000 men (or 100,000 inclusive of the government functionaries), under the direct leadership of the Central Committee of the Communist Party, started from the central base on the Long March, leaving only a small force led by Chen Yi and other comrades in the base to carry out guerrilla warfare and cover the main force in its break through the encirclement. After breaching four blockade lines formed by 400,000 enemy troops, the First Front Army arrived at the border of Hunan and Kwangsi in November 1934 and pushed towards the Hunan-Hupeh-Szechuan-Kweichow base set up by the Second Front Army. Chiang Kai-shek, in mortal fear of the joining of forces of the two main units of the Red Army, hurriedly mustered a force about six times as large as the Red Army to intercept the latter in western Hunan. He also ordered the Kwangsi warlords to attack the Red Army from northern Kwangsi, trying to surround and annihilate the First Front Army. The situation looked grave. Because of the firm stand of Comrade Mao Tsetung and the support of a majority of the leading comrades, the First Front Army altered its course and advanced towards Kweichow where the enemy defence was weak, quickly occupying eastern Kweichow. In January 1935 it crossed the Wu River, a natural barrier, and captured Tsunyi, the biggest city of northern Kweichow. There it took a rest of 12 days, during which period it replenished its ranks with about five thousand new fighters. The Communist Party also called an enlarged meeting of the Central Political Bureau — the Tsûnyi Conference — which had great significance in the history of the Chinese revolution.

Having caused the Red Army to suffer defeat by carrying out an incorrect policy during the fight against Chiang Kai-shek's fifth encirclement campaign, the com-

rades who had committed "Left" mistakes became frightened. They failed to do a good job of political agitation
at the beginning of the Long March. Then, during the
Long March, their sole thought was to steer clear of the
enemy, with the result that the Red Army was often
made to fulfil a passive role, and morale suffered. They
also formed over-large commanding and logistical organizations which slowed down the movement of the troops.
Blockaded and pursued by the enemy, the Red Army was
more than once in a precarious position. By the time it
reached Tsunyi in January 1935, the First Front Army had
suffered a loss of 60 per cent of its men.

This serious situation, contrasted with the previous
victory in crushing the enemy's fourth campaign of encirclement, could not but open the eyes of a majority of
the leading members and rank-and-file members in the
Party to the fact that things had gone wrong as a result
of rejection of the correct line represented by Comrade
Mao Tsetung in favour of the erroneous line. Doubts and
discontent arose among the troops and they demanded a
change in the leading personnel. Led by Comrade Mao
Tsetung, a resolute struggle was waged against the "Left"
opportunist line and it culminated in the Tsunyi Conference which put an end to the domination of the "Left"
line in the Party Centre and established the correct leadership of the Central Committee headed by Comrade Mao
Tsetung. Thus the Party and the Red Army were saved
from an imminent danger. The Tsunyi Conference marks
a turning-point of historic significance which made it possible for the Party to bring the Long March successfully

to the end, and preserve and steel the backbones of the Party and the Red Army at time of trial during the Long March.

After the Tsunyi Conference, the First Front Army, under the wise leadership of Comrade Mao Tsetung, adopted flexible tactics, taking the initiative into its own hands. In February 1935, it wiped out four enemy divisions near Tsunyi and won the first great victory since the beginning of the Long March. After this, the First Front Army, confusing the enemy by feints, succeeded in giving him the slip. It crossed the swift Golden Sand River on the border of Szechuan and Yunnan in a matter of nine days and nine nights in May — without suffering any loss.

The Red Army had broken through the blockade of hundreds of thousands of enemy troops. This was the decisive victory of the Long March. From that time onwards, the Red Army went north along western Szechuan, forced the Tatu River, scaled the Great Snow Mountain Range and reached Tawei and Maokung in western Szechuan in June 1935, joining forces with the Fourth Front Army in the Szechuan-Shensi base.

Chang Kuo-tao, one of the leaders of the Fourth Front Army, lost confidence in the prospects of the revolution after the failure of the fifth anti-encirclement campaign and pursued the Right opportunist runaway policy. In March 1935, he abandoned the Szechuan-Shensi base and moved his troops westwards, intending to withdraw — flee, actually — towards southwest China. After crossing the Chialing, Fu and Min Rivers to the west, these troops

joined forces with the First Front Army in the area of
Lihsien and Maokung.

Comrade Mao Tsetung had applied the correct line of
inner-Party struggle towards Chang Kuo-tao's errors. In
order to get him round by patient persuasion, the Party
Central Committee called an important meeting at Sung-
pan in the northwest of Szechuan, which, following discussion, decided that the Red Army was to continue its
march northwards. Finally, Chang Kuo-tao accepted
nominally the decision by the Central Committee.

In August 1935, the Red Army continued to march
north in two columns — the right led by the Central Committee of the Party and Comrade Mao Tsetung; the left
by Chu Teh, Chang Kuo-tao and Liu Po-cheng. However, when the left column reached Apa (now in the Apa
Tibetan Autonomous *Chou* in Szechuan), Chang Kuo-tao
again refused to carry out the decision of the Central
Committee and, detaining Chu Teh and Liu Po-cheng,
took the troops south. He also secretly ordered the two
armies of the Fourth Front Army, which had been put
under the right column, to go south with him and retreat
to Tienchuan and Lushan (now north of Yaan in Szechuan). Later, he openly raised slogans against the Central Committee, and even plotted to destroy it. The
Central Committee then decided to continue to lead the
right column north alone. In September, they captured
the natural barrier of Latsekou on the border of Szechuan
and Kansu, crossed Mount Min and entered southern
Kansu. In the following month, they reached Wuchi
Town in northern Shensi and joined forces with the 15th

Army Corps then manoeuvring in northern Shensi. In November, the two Red Army units together repulsed the pursuing enemy troops and consolidated the Shensi-Kansu base, which later developed into the famous Shensi-Kansu-Ningsia Border Region with Yenan as its centre.

In November 1935, the Second Front Army, having fulfilled its task of covering the First Front Army in the Long March by carrying out guerrilla warfare in the enemy's rear, set out on the Long March itself, following approximately the same route traversed by the First Front Army. In June 1936, it reached Kantse in western Szechuan and joined forces with the Fourth Front Army led by Chang Kuo-tao which was biding its time there.

Now that Chang Kuo-tao who harboured sinister intentions had gone to the length of turning traitor to the Party, he set up a bogus "party centre" and made himself chairman. He tried to incite the leaders of the Second Front Army to join him in opposing the Party Central Committee and support his runaway policy and anti-Party splittist activities. Adhering to Comrade Mao Tsetung's correct line of inner-Party struggle, Comrade Chu Teh displayed firm political integrity and revolutionary qualities by rejecting Chang Kuo-tao's request for a declaration against the Party Central Committee and, what was more, propagating among the cadres the correct line of the Central Committee. Thanks to the resolute support of Comrades Chu Teh, Liu Po-cheng, Jen Pi-shih and Kuan Hsiang-ying (the last two being leaders of the Second Front Army) to the correct line of the Party Central Committee and their struggle against Chang Kuo-tao's runaway policy and anti-Party splittist activities, and because of the awakening of the bulk of the Fourth Front Army cadres to the error of Chang Kuo-tao's line and their demand for continued advance northwards to resist Japan, Chang Kuo-tao's traitorous splittist schemes ended in failure. He was compelled to disband his bogus "party centre" and, in July, lead the Fourth Front Army northwards together with the Second. They reached Huining in Kansu in October and joined forces with the First Front Army. With the meeting of the three main forces of the Red Army — the First, Second and Fourth Front Armies — the Long March was triumphantly brought to an end.

The Long March is a great epic unexampled in Chinese history. The farthest distance covered by the Red Army was 25,000 *li*, extending, in terms of order, over Fukien, Kiangsi, Kwangtung, Hunan, Kwangsi, Kweichow, Yunnan, Sikang, Szechuan, Kansu and Shensi, eleven provinces all told. Chiang Kai-shek had exerted his utmost efforts to mobilize his crack army and air force units, work together with the troops of warlords and landlords' armed forces in various provinces, and set up defence works at natural barriers along the route of advance of the Red Army, while never letting up in his attacks. To avoid an enemy which was far better equipped and in much greater numbers, the Red Army had to advance over desolate regions, crossing lofty mountains and turbulent rivers, dangerous shoals and paths, particularly in western

Szechuan, with its snow-capped mountains rising 5,000 metres above sea level, and its treacherous marshlands. These regions were marked by their general poverty and sparse population and shortage of food.

None of these difficulties and hazards, however, prevented the Red Army from achieving victory in the Long March. That was because, first and foremost, the Red Army was led by a Marxist-Leninist Party, the Chinese Communist Party. Since its founding in 1921, the Party, tempered in long revolutionary struggles, had learned to integrate Marxist-Leninist theory with the revolutionary practice of China, had accumulated much experience, particularly the experience of revolutionary wars, and had trained a large number of leading personnel. After the Tsunyi Conference, the Central Committee of the Party headed by Comrade Mao Tsetung was established, which carried out a correct line. Not only was it adept at struggling with all kinds of enemies; it was adept also at struggling against erroneous tendencies within the Party. The whole course of the Long March bears out that its victory was achieved through the complete rectification of the "Left" erroneous line and the establishment of the leadership of Comrade Mao Tsetung's correct line, through the resolute struggle against Chang Kuo-tao's Right opportunist line and splittist schemes, and through adherence to Comrade Mao Tsetung's correct views. The victory of the Long March of the Red Army would have been inconceivable without the correct leadership of the Party and Comrade Mao Tsetung.

Comrade Mao Tsetung has elaborated in vivid terms the significance of the Long March as follows:

Speaking of the Long March, one may ask, "What is its significance?" We answer that the Long March is the first of its kind in the annals of history, that it is a manifesto. . . . It has proclaimed to the world that the Red Army is an army of heroes, while the imperialists and their running dogs, Chiang Kai-shek and his like, are impotent. It has proclaimed their utter failure to encircle, pursue, obstruct and intercept us. The Long March is also a propaganda force. It has announced to some 200 million people in eleven provinces that the road of the Red Army is their only road to liberation. Without the Long March, how could the broad masses have learned so quickly about the existence of the great truth which the Red Army embodies? The Long March is also a seeding-machine. In the eleven provinces it has sown many seeds which will sprout, leaf, blossom, and bear fruit, and will yield a harvest in the future. In a word, the Long March has ended with victory for us and defeat for the enemy.

("On Tactics Against Japanese Imperialism")

The victorious conclusion of the Long March enabled the Chinese revolution to tide over another crisis after that of 1927. It inspired the entire Chinese people with confidence in the prospects of their revolution and War of Resistance Against Japan. It preserved the crack force of the Chinese Communist Party and the Red Army, and steeled the Party ranks through severe ordeals. It was thanks to this force that the revolutionary strength during the anti-Japanese war grew stronger than ever before under the correct leadership of the Party and Comrade Mao Tsetung and thus laid the foundation for the great victory won by the Chinese people in overthrowing the rule of imperialism and its running dogs, Kuomintang reactionaries, and bringing a new China into being.

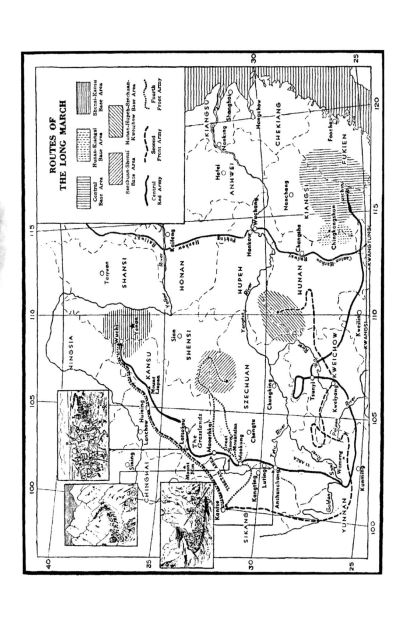

ROUTES OF
THE LONG MARCH

Central
Base Area

Hunan-Kiangsi
Base Area

Szechuan-Shensi
Base Area

Shensi-Kansu
Base Area

Hunan-Hupeh-Szechuan-
Kweichow Base Area

Central
Red Army

Second
Front Army

Fourth
Front Army

Printed in the United States
28593LVS00001B/61